Preface

Microsoft Azure Developer AZ 204: Developing Solutions for Microsoft Azure is a comprehensive guide meticulously designed to equip developers with the essential knowledge and practical skills required to build, deploy, and manage cloud-based applications on Microsoft Azure. As cloud computing continues to be a driving force behind technological advancements across industries, proficiency in Azure development has become indispensable for modern software engineers. This book is structured to align with the objectives of the AZ-204 certification, covering fundamental and advanced topics such as implementing compute solutions, developing Azure Functions, integrating Azure storage, and managing application security and identity solutions. Through a well-organized progression of topics, this guide ensures that readers acquire a solid understanding of Azure development principles while gaining hands-on experience with real-world scenarios and industry best practices.

Beyond serving as a certification preparation resource, Microsoft Certification AZ-204: Developing Solutions for Microsoft Azure is a valuable reference for professionals aiming to enhance their cloud development expertise. Each chapter includes practical exercises, self-assessment tools, and review questions to reinforce learning and ensure readiness for the AZ-204 exam. Additionally, supplementary resources such as online test papers and expert-led video tutorials provide an immersive learning experience, bridging the gap between theoretical knowledge and practical implementation. Whether you are an aspiring Azure developer or an experienced professional seeking to validate and expand your cloud computing skills, this book offers a structured and in-depth approach to mastering Azure development, paving the way for career growth and technical excellence in the ever-evolving cloud ecosystem.

Table of Contents

Preface 1
Chapter 1: Practice Questions & Answers Part 1 3
Chapter 2: Practice Questions & Answers Part 2 41
Chapter 3: Viva Voce Questions 79

Chapter 1: Practice Questions & Answers Part 1

QUESTION 1

-

You need to resolve the Shipping web site error.
How should you configure the Azure Table Storage service? To answer, select the appropriate options in the answer area. NOTE: Each correct selection is worth one point.
A. Mastered
B. Not Mastered
Answer: A

QUESTION 2

-

You need to update the APIs to resolve the testing error.
How should you complete the Azure CLI command? To answer, select the appropriate options in the answer area. NOTE: Each correct selection is worth one point.
A. Mastered
B. Not Mastered
Answer: A

QUESTION 3

-

You need to ensure that validation testing is triggered per the requirements.
How should you complete the code segment? To answer, select the appropriate values in the answer area. NOTE: Each correct selection is worth one point.
A. Mastered
B. Not Mastered
Answer: A

QUESTION 4

-

You need to investigate the http server log output to resolve the issue with the ContentUploadService. Which command should you use first?
A. az webapp log
B. az ams live-output
C. az monitor activity-log
D. az container attach
Answer: C

QUESTION 5

-

You need to add code at line AM09 to ensure that users can review content using ContentAnalysisService. How should you complete the code? To answer, select the appropriate options in the answer area.
NOTE: Each correct selection is worth one point.

A. Mastered
B. Not Mastered
Answer: A

QUESTION 6

-

You need to retrieve the database connection string.
Which values should you use? To answer, select the appropriate options in the answer area. NOTE: Each correct selection is worth one point.
A. Mastered
B. Not Mastered
Answer: A

QUESTION 7

-

You need to configure security and compliance for the corporate website files.
Which Azure Blob storage settings should you use? To answer, select the appropriate options in the answer area. NOTE: Each correct selection is worth one point.
A. Mastered
B. Not Mastered
Answer: A

QUESTION 8

-

You need to ensure that all messages from Azure Event Grid are processed. What should you use?
A. Azure Event Grid topic
B. Azure Service Bus topic
C. Azure Service Bus queue
D. Azure Storage queue
E. Azure Logic App custom connector
Answer: B

QUESTION 9

-

You need to implement the Log policy.
How should you complete the EnsureLogging method in EventGridController.cs? To answer, select the appropriate options in the answer area. NOTE: Each correct selection is worth one point.
A. Mastered
B. Not Mastered
Answer: A

QUESTION 10

-

You need to ensure that PolicyLib requirements are met.

How should you complete the code segment? To answer, drag the appropriate code segments to the correct locations. Each code segment may be used once, more than once, or not at all. You may need to drag the split bar between panes or scroll to view content.
NOTE: Each correct selection is worth one point.
A. Mastered
B. Not Mastered
Answer: A

QUESTION 11

-

You need to add code at line PC26 of Processing.cs to ensure that security policies are met.
How should you complete the code that you will add at line PC26? To answer, select the appropriate options in the answer area. NOTE: Each correct selection is worth one point
A. Mastered
B. Not Mastered
Answer: A

QUESTION 12

-

You need to retrieve all order line items from Order.json and sort the data alphabetically by the city. How should you complete the code? To answer, select the appropriate options in the answer area. NOTE: Each correct selection is worth one point.
A. Mastered
B. Not Mastered
Answer: A

QUESTION 13

-

A company has multiple warehouse. Each warehouse contains IoT temperature devices which deliver temperature data to an Azure Service Bus queue. You need to send email alerts to facility supervisors immediately if the temperature at a warehouse goes above or below specified threshold temperatures.
Which five actions should you perform in sequence? To answer, move the appropriate actions from the list of actions to the answer area and arrange them in the correct order.
A. Mastered
B. Not Mastered
Answer: A

QUESTION 14

-

You are developing applications for a company. You plan to host the applications on Azure App Services. The company has the following requirements:
Every five minutes verify that the websites are responsive.
Verify that the websites respond within a specified time threshold. Dependent requests such as images and JavaScript files must load properly. Generate alerts if a website is experiencing issues.

If a website fails to load, the system must attempt to reload the site three more times. You need to implement this process with the least amount of effort. What should you do? D18912E1457D5D1DDCBD40AB3BF70D5D

A. Create a Selenium web test and configure it to run from your workstation as a scheduled task.
B. Set up a URL ping test to query the home page.
C. Create an Azure function to query the home page.
D. Create a multi-step web test to query the home page.
E. Create a Custom Track Availability Test to query the home page.

Answer: D

QUESTION 15

-

Note: This question is part of a series of questions that present the same scenario. Each question in the series contains a unique solution that might meet the stated goals. Some question sets might have more than one correct solution, while others might not have a correct solution.

After you answer a question in this section, you will NOT be able to return to it. As a result, these questions will not appear in the review screen. You develop Azure solutions.

You must grant a virtual machine (VM) access to specific resource groups in Azure Resource Manager. You need to obtain an Azure Resource Manager access token.

Solution: Use an X.509 certificate to authenticate the VM with Azure Resource Manager. Does the solution meet the goal?

A. Yes
B. No

Answer: B

QUESTION 16

-

You are developing an Azure Function app. The app must meet the following requirements: Enable developers to write the functions by using the Rust language. Declaratively connect to an Azure Blob Storage account.

You need to implement the app.

Which Azure Function app features should you use? To answer, drag the appropriate features to the correct requirements. Each feature may be used once, more than once, or not at all. You may need to drag the split bar between panes or scroll to view content.

NOTE: Each correct selection is worth one point.

A. Mastered
B. Not Mastered

Answer: A

QUESTION 17

-

Note: This question is part of a series of questions that present the same scenario. Each question in the series contains a unique solution that might meet the stated goals. Some question sets might have more than one correct solution, while others might not have a correct solution.

After you answer a question in this section, you will NOT be able to return to it. As a result, these questions will not appear in the review screen. Margie's Travel is an international travel and

bookings management service. The company is expanding into restaurant bookings. You are tasked with implementing Azure Search for the restaurants listed in their solution
You create the index in Azure Search.
You need to import the restaurant data into the Azure Search service by using the Azure Search NET SDK. Solution:
* 1. Create a SearchIndexClient object to connect to the search index
* 2. Create an IndexBatch that contains the documents which must be added.
* 3. Call the Documents.Index method of the SearchIndexClient and pass the IndexBatch. Does the solution meet the goal?
A. Yes
B. No
Answer: A

QUESTION 18

-

You are developing an Azure Function App that processes images that are uploaded to an Azure Blob container.
Images must be processed as quickly as possible after they are uploaded, and the solution must minimize latency. You create code to process images when the Function App is triggered.
You need to configure the Function App. What should you do?
A. Use an App Service pla
B. Configure the Function App to use an Azure Blob Storage input trigger.
C. Use a Consumption pla
D. Configure the Function App to use an Azure Blob Storage trigger.
E. Use a Consumption pla
F. Configure the Function App to use a Timer trigger.
G. Use an App Service pla
H. Configure the Function App to use an Azure Blob Storage trigger.
I. Use a Consumption pla
J. Configure the Function App to use an Azure Blob Storage input trigger.
Answer: B

QUESTION 19

-

You are building a traffic monitoring system that monitors traffic along six highways. The system produces time series analysis-based reports for each highway. Data from traffic sensors are stored in Azure Event Hub.
Traffic data is consumed by four departments. Each department has an Azure Web App that displays the time-series-based reports and contains a WebJob that processes the incoming data from Event Hub. All Web Apps run on App Service Plans with three instances.
Data throughout must be maximized. Latency must be minimized. You need to implement the Azure Event Hub. Which settings should you use? To answer, select the appropriate options in the answer area.
NOTE: Each correct selection is worth one point.
A. Mastered
B. Not Mastered

Answer: A

QUESTION 20

-

You are developing a solution for a hospital to support the following use cases:
•The most recent patient status details must be retrieved even if multiple users in different locations have updated the patient record.
•Patient health monitoring data retrieved must be the current version or the prior version.
•After a patient is discharged and all charges have been assessed, the patient billing record contains the final charges.
You provision a Cosmos DB NoSQL database and set the default consistency level for the database account to Strong. You set the value for Indexing Mode to Consistent.
You need to minimize latency and any impact to the availability of the solution. You must override the default consistency level at the query level to meet the required consistency guarantees for the scenarios.
Which consistency levels should you implement? To answer, drag the appropriate consistency levels to the correct requirements. Each consistency level may be used once, more than once, or not at all. You may need to drag the split bar between panes or scroll to view content.
NOTE: Each correct selection is worth one point.
A. Mastered
B. Not Mastered
Answer: A

QUESTION 21

-

You are implementing a software as a service (SaaS) ASP.NET Core web service that will run as an Azure Web App. The web service will use an on-premises SQL Server database for storage. The web service also includes a WebJob that processes data updates. Four customers will use the web service.
•Each instance of the WebJob processes data for a single customer and must run as a singleton instance.
•Each deployment must be tested by using deployment slots prior to serving production data.
•Azure costs must be minimized.
•Azure resources must be located in an isolated network. You need to configure the App Service plan for the Web App.
How should you configure the App Service plan? To answer, select the appropriate settings in the answer area. NOTE: Each correct selection is worth one point.
A. Mastered
B. Not Mastered
Answer: A

QUESTION 22

-

You are developing an ASP.NET Core Web API web service that uses Azure Application Insights to monitor performance and track events. You need to enable logging and ensure that log messages can be correlated to events tracked by Application Insights.

How should you complete the code? To answer, drag the appropriate code segments to the correct locations. Each code segment may be used once, more than once, or not at all. You may need to drag the split bar between panes or scroll to view content.
NOTE: Each correct selection is worth one point.
A. Mastered
B. Not Mastered
Answer: A

QUESTION 23

-

A company develops a series of mobile games. All games use a single leaderboard service. You have the following requirements:
•Code should be scalable and allow for growth.
•Each record must consist of a playedId, gameId, score, and time played.
•When users reach a new high score, the system will save the new score using the SaveScore function below.
•Each game is assigned and Id based on the series title.
You have the following code. (Line numbers are included for reference only.)
You store customer information in an Azure Cosmos database. The following data already exists in the database:
For each of the following statements, select Yes if the statement is true. Otherwise, select No.
NOTE: Each correct selection is worth one point.
A. Mastered
B. Not Mastered
Answer: A

QUESTION 24

-

You are developing an Azure solution.
You need to develop code to access a secret stored in Azure Key Vault.
How should you complete the code segment? To answer, drag the appropriate code segments to the correct locations. Each code segment may be used once, more than once, or not at all. You may need to drag the split bar between panes or scroll to view content.
NOTE: Each correct selection is worth one point.
A. Mastered
B. Not Mastered
Answer: A

QUESTION 25

-

Note: This question is part of a series of questions that present the same scenario. Each question in the series contains a unique solution that might meet the stated goals. Some question sets might have more than one correct solution, while others might not have a correct solution.
After you answer a question in this section, you will NOT be able to return to it. As a result, these questions will not appear in the review screen.

You are developing an Azure Service application that processes queue data when it receives a message from a mobile application. Messages may not be sent to the service consistently.
You have the following requirements:
Queue size must not grow larger than 80 gigabytes (GB). Use first-in-first-out (FIFO) ordering of messages.
Minimize Azure costs.
You need to implement the messaging solution.
Solution: Use the .Net API to add a message to an Azure Storage Queue from the mobile application. Create an Azure Function App that uses an Azure Storage Queue trigger.
Does the solution meet the goal?
A. Yes
B. No
Answer: B

QUESTION 26

-

You develop a web app that uses tier D1 app service plan by using the Web Apps feature of Microsoft Azure App Service. Spikes in traffic have caused increases in page load times.
You need to ensure that the web app automatically scales when CPU load is about 85 percent and minimize costs.
Which four actions should you perform in sequence? To answer, move the appropriate actions from the list of actions to the answer area and arrange them in the correct order.
NOTE: More than one order of answer choices is correct. You will receive credit for any of the correct orders you select.
A. Mastered
B. Not Mastered
Answer: A

QUESTION 27

-

You develop a gateway solution for a public facing news API.
The news API back end is implemented as a RESTful service and hosted in an Azure App Service instance. You need to configure back-end authentication for the API Management service instance.
Which target and gateway credential type should you use? To answer, drag the appropriate values to the correct parameters. Each value may be used once, more than once, or not at all. You may need to drag the split bar between panes or scroll to view content.
NOTE: Each correct selection is worth one point.
A. Mastered
B. Not Mastered
Answer: A

QUESTION 28

-

You use Azure Table storage to store customer information for an application. The data contains customer details and is partitioned by last name. You need to create a query that returns all customers with the last name Smith. Which code segment should you use?

A. TableQuery.GenerateFilterCondition("PartitionKey", Equals, "Smith")
B. TableQuery.GenerateFilterCondition("LastName", Equals, "Smith")
C. TableQuery.GenerateFilterCondition("PartitionKey", QueryComparisons.Equal, "Smith")
D. TableQuery.GenerateFilterCondition("LastName", QueryComparisons.Equal, "Smith")
Answer: C

QUESTION 29

-

You are writing code to create and run an Azure Batch job. You have created a pool of compute nodes.
You need to choose the right class and its method to submit a batch job to the Batch service. Which method should you use?
A. JobOperations.CreateJobO
B. CloudJob.Enable(IEnumerable<BatchClientBehavior>)
C. CloudJob.CommitAsync(IEnumerable<BatchClientBehavior>, CancellationToken)
D. JobOperations.EnableJob(String, IEnumerable<BatchClientBehavior>)
E. JobOperations.EnableJobAsync(Strin
F. IEnumerable<BatchClientBehavior>. CancellationToken)
Answer: C

QUESTION 30

-

You develop and deploy an ASP.NET web app to Azure App Service. You use Application Insights telemetry to monitor the app.
You must test the app to ensure that the app is available and responsive from various points around the world and at regular intervals. If the app is not responding, you must send an alert to support staff.You need to configure a test for the web app.
Which two test types can you use? Each correct answer presents a complete solution. NOTE: Each correct selection is worth one point.
A. integration
B. multi-step web
C. URL ping
D. unit
E. load
Answer: BC

QUESTION 31

-

You are developing an Azure-hosted e-commerce web application. The application will use Azure Cosmos DB to store sales orders. You are using the latest SDK to manage the sales orders in the database.
You create a new Azure Cosmos DB instance. You include a valid endpoint and valid authorization key to an appSettings.json file in the code project. You are evaluating the following application code: (Line number are included for reference only.)
For each of the following statements, select Yes if the statement is true. Otherwise, select No. NOTE: Each correct selection is worth one point.

A. Mastered
B. Not Mastered
Answer: A

QUESTION 32

-

You are developing an Azure Cosmos DB solution by using the Azure Cosmos DB SQL API. The data includes millions of documents. Each document may contain hundreds of properties.
The properties of the documents do not contain distinct values for partitioning. Azure Cosmos DB must scale individual containers in the database to meet the performance needs of the application by spreading the workload evenly across all partitions over time.
You need to select a partition key.
Which two partition keys can you use? Each correct answer presents a complete solution. NOTE: Each correct selection is worth one point.
A. a concatenation of multiple property values with a random suffix appended
B. a single property value that does not appear frequently in the documents
C. a hash suffix appended to a property value
D. a value containing the collection name
E. a single property value that appears frequently in the documents
Answer: AC

QUESTION 33

-

You have an application that includes an Azure Web app and several Azure Function apps. Application secrets including connection strings and certificates are stored in Azure Key Vault. Secrets must not be stored in the application or application runtime environment. Changes to Azure Active Directory (Azure AD) must be minimized. You need to design the approach to loading application secrets. What should you do?

A. Create a single user-assigned Managed Identity with permission to access Key Vault and configure each App Service to use that Managed Identity.
B. Create a single Azure AD Service Principal with permission to access Key Vault and use a client secret from within the App Services to access Key Vault.
C. Create a system assigned Managed Identity in each App Service with permission to access Key Vault.
D. Create an Azure AD Service Principal with Permissions to access Key Vault for each App Service and use a certificate from within the App Services to access Key Vault.
Answer: C

QUESTION 34

-

Note: This question is part of a series of questions that present the same scenario. Each question in the series contains a unique solution that might meet the stated goals. Some question sets might have more than one correct solution, while others might not have a correct solution.
After you answer a question in this section, you will NOT be able to return to it. As a result, these questions will not appear in the review screen. Margie's Travel is an international travel and

bookings management service. The company is expanding into restaurant bookings. You are tasked with implementing Azure Search tor the restaurants listed in their solution.
You create the index in Azure Search.
You need to import the restaurant data into the Azure Search service by using the Azure Search NET SDK. Solution:
* 1. Create a SearchServiceClient object to connect to the search index.
* 2. Create a DataContainer that contains the documents which must be added.
* 3. Create a DataSource instance and set its Container property to the DataContainer.
* 4. Set the DataSource property of the SearchServiceClient Does the solution meet the goal?
A. Yes
B. No
Answer: B

QUESTION 35

-

You are developing a .NET Core MVC application for customers to research hotels. The application will use Azure Search. The application will search the index by using various criteria to locate documents related to hotels. The index will include search fields for rate, a list of amenities, and distance to the nearest airport.
The application must support the following scenarios for specifying search criteria and organizing results:

- Search the index by using regular expressions.
- Organize results by counts for name-value pairs.
- List hotels within a specified distance to an airport and that fall within a specific price range. You need to configure the SearchParameters class. Which properties should you configure? To answer, select the appropriate options in the answer area. NOTE Each correct selection is worth one point.

A. Mastered
B. Not Mastered
Answer: A

QUESTION 36

-

You are developing a software solution for an autonomous transportation system. The solution uses large data sets and Azure Batch processing to simulate navigation sets for entire fleets of vehicles.
You need to create compute nodes for the solution on Azure Batch. What should you do?
A. In Python, implement the class: TaskAddParameter
B. In Python, implement the class: JobAddParameter
C. In the Azure portal, create a Batch account
D. In a .NET method, call the method: BatchClient.PoolOperations.CreateJob
Answer: D

QUESTION 37

-

You are developing a ticket reservation system for an airline.

The storage solution for the application must meet the following requirements:
Ensure at least 99.99% availability and provide low latency.
Accept reservations event when localized network outages or other unforeseen failures occur.
Process reservations in the exact sequence as reservations are submitted to minimize overbooking or selling the same seat to multiple travelers.
Allow simultaneous and out-of-order reservations with a maximum five-second tolerance window.
You provision a resource group named airlineResourceGroup in the Azure South-Central US region. You need to provision a SQL SPI Cosmos DB account to support the app.
How should you complete the Azure CLI commands? To answer, select the appropriate options in the answer area. NOTE: Each correct selection is worth one point.
A. Mastered
B. Not Mastered
Answer: A

QUESTION 38

-

You are creating a hazard notification system that has a single signaling server which triggers audio and visual alarms to start and stop.You implement Azure Service Bus to publish alarms. Each alarm controller uses Azure Service Bus to receive alarm signals as part of a transaction. Alarm events must be recorded for audit purposes. Each transaction record must include information about the alarm type that was activated.
You need to implement a reply trail auditing solution.
Which two actions should you perform? Each correct answer presents part of the solution. NOTE: Each correct selection is worth one point.
A. Assign the value of the hazard message SessionID property to the ReplyToSessionld property.
B. Assign the value of the hazard message Messageld property to the DevileryCount property.
C. Assign the value of the hazard message SessionID property to the SequenceNumber property.
D. Assign the value of the hazard message Messageld property to the Correlationld property.
E. Assign the value of the hazard message SequenceNumber property to the DeliveryCount property.
F. Assign the value of the hazard message Messageld property to the SequenceNumber property.
Answer: AD

QUESTION 39

-

Note: This question is part of a series of questions that present the same scenario. Each question in the series contains a unique solution that might meet the stated goals. Some question sets might have more than one correct solution, while others might not have a correct solution.
After you answer a question in this section, you will NOT be able to return to it. As a result, these questions will not appear in the review screen.
You develop and deploy an Azure App Service API app to a Windows-hosted deployment slot named Development. You create additional deployment slots named Testing and Production. You enable auto swap on the Production deployment slot.
You need to ensure that scripts run and resources are available before a swap operation occurs.
Solution: Update the app with a method named statuscheck to run the scripts. Update the app settings for the app. Set the WEBSITE_SWAP_WARMUP_PING_PATH and

WEBSITE_SWAP_WARMUP_PING_STATUSES with a path to the new method and appropriate response codes. Does the solution meet the goal?
A. Yes
B. No
Answer: B

QUESTION 40

-

A company is implementing a publish-subscribe (Pub/Sub) messaging component by using Azure Service Bus. You are developing the first subscription application.
In the Azure portal you see that messages are being sent to the subscription for each topic. You create and initialize a subscription client object by supplying the correct details, but the subscription application is still not consuming the messages.
You need to complete the source code of the subscription client What should you do?
A. await subscriptionClient.CloseAsync();
B. await subscriptionClient.AddRuleAsync(new RuleDescription(RuleDescription.DefaultRuleName, new TrueFilter()));
C. subscriptionClient.RegisterMessageHandler(ProcessMessagesAsync, messageHandlerOptions);
D. subscriptionClient = new SubscriptionClient(ServiceBusConnectionString, TopicName, SubscriptionName);
Answer: C

QUESTION 41

-

Note: This question is part of a series of questions that present the same scenario. Each question in the series contains a unique solution that might meet the stated goals. Some question sets might have more than one correct solution, while others might not have a correct solution.
After you answer a question in this section, you will NOT be able to return to it. As a result, these questions will not appear in the review screen.
You are developing a website that will run as an Azure Web App. Users will authenticate by using their Azure Active Directory (Azure AD) credentials.
You plan to assign users one of the following permission levels for the website: admin, normal, and reader. A user's Azure AD group membership must be used to determine the permission level.
You need to configure authorization. Solution:
Create a new Azure AD application. In the application's manifest, define application roles that match the required permission levels for the application. Assign the appropriate Azure AD group to each role. In the website, use the value of the roles claim from the JWT for the user to determine permissions. Does the solution meet the goal?
A. Yes
B. No
Answer: B

QUESTION 42

-

You have a single page application (SPA) web application that manages information based on data returned by Microsoft Graph from another company's Azure Active Directory (Azure AD) instance.
Users must be able to authenticate and access Microsoft Graph by using their own company's Azure AD instance. You need to configure the application manifest for the app registration.
How should you complete the manifest? To answer, select the appropriate options in the answer area. NOTE: Each correct selection is worth one point.
A. Mastered
B. Not Mastered
Answer: A

QUESTION 43

-

You are developing a new page for a website that uses Azure Cosmos DB for data storage. The feature uses documents that have the following format:
You must display data for the new page in a specific order. You create the following query for the page:
You need to configure a Cosmos DB policy to the support the query.
How should you configure the policy? To answer, drag the appropriate JSON segments to the correct locations. Each JSON segment may be used once, more than once, or not at all. You may need to drag the split bar between panes or scroll to view content.
NOTE: Each correct selection is worth one point.
A. Mastered
B. Not Mastered
Answer: A

QUESTION 44

-

You are implementing an order processing system. A point of sale application publishes orders to topics in an Azure Service Bus queue. The label property for the topic includes the following data:
The system has the following requirements for subscriptions
You need to implement filtering and maximize throughput while evaluating filters.
Which filter types should you implement? To answer, drag the appropriate filter types to the correct subscriptions. Each filter type may be used once, more than once, or not at all. You may need to drag the split bar between panes or scroll to view content.
NOTE: Each correct selection is worth one point.
A. Mastered
B. Not Mastered
Answer: A

QUESTION 45

-

You are developing an ASP.NET Core website that can be used to manage photographs which are stored in Azure Blob Storage containers. Users of the website authenticate by using their Azure Active Directory (Azure AD) credentials.

You implement role-based access control (RBAC) role permission on the containers that store photographs. You assign users to RBAC role.
You need to configure the website's Azure AD Application so that user's permissions can be used with the Azure Blob containers.
How should you configure the application? To answer, drag the appropriate setting to the correct location. Each setting may be used once, more than once, or not at all. You may need to drag the split bar between panes or scroll to view content.
NOTE: Each correct selection is worth one point.
A. Mastered
B. Not Mastered
Answer: A

QUESTION 46

-

Note: This question is part of a series of questions that present the same scenario. Each question in the series contains a unique solution that might meet the stated goals. Some question sets might have more than one correct solution, while others might not have a correct solution.
After you answer a question in this section, you will NOT be able to return to it. As a result these questions will not appear in the review screen. Margie's Travel is an international travel and bookings management service. The company is expanding into restaurant bookings. You are tasked with implementing Azure Search for the restaurants listed in their solution.
You create the index in Azure Search.
You need to import the restaurant data into the Azure Search service by using the Azure Search .NET SDK. Solution:
* 1. Create a SearchlndexClient object to connect to the search index.
* 2. Create a DataContainer that contains the documents which must be added.
* 3. Create a DataSource instance and set its Container property to the DataContamer
* 4 Call the Documents.Suggest method of the SearchlndexClient and pass the DataSource. Does the solution meet the goal?

A. Yes
B. No
Answer: B

QUESTION 47

-

Note: This question is part of a series of questions that present the same scenario. Each question in the series contains a unique solution that might meet the stated goals. Some question sets might have more than one correct solution, while others might not have a correct solution.
After you answer a question in this section, you will NOT be able to return to it. As a result, these questions will not appear in the review screen.
You develop a software as a service (SaaS) offering to manage photographs. Users upload photos to a web service which then stores the photos in Azure Storage Blob storage. The storage account type is
General-purpose V2.

When photos are uploaded, they must be processed to produce and save a mobile-friendly version of the image. The process to produce a mobile-friendly version of the image must start in less than one minute.
You need to design the process that starts the photo processing.
Solution: Move photo processing to an Azure Function triggered from the blob upload. Does the solution meet the goal?
A. Yes
B. No
Answer: A

QUESTION 48

-

You are developing a web service that will run on Azure virtual machines that use Azure Storage. You configure all virtual machines to use managed identities. You have the following requirements:
Must use only Azure Instance Metadata Service endpoints.
You need to write code to retrieve an access token to access Azure Storage. To answer, drag the appropriate code segments to the correct locations. Each code segment may be used once or not at all. You may need to drag the split bar between panes or scroll to view content.
NOTE: Each correct selection is worth one point
A. Mastered
B. Not Mastered
Answer: A

QUESTION 49

-

Note: This question is part of a series of questions that present the same scenario. Each question in the series contains a unique solution. Determine whether the solution meets the stated goals.
You are developing and deploying several ASP.Net web applications to Azure App Service. You plan to save session state information and HTML output. You must use a storage mechanism with the following requirements:
•Share session state across all ASP.NET web applications
•Support controlled, concurrent access to the same session state data for multiple readers and a single writer
•Save full HTTP responses for concurrent requests You need to store the information.
Proposed Solution: Deploy and configure an Azure Database for PostgreSQL. Update the web applications. Does the solution meet the goal?
A. Yes
B. No
Answer: B

QUESTION 50

-

You have an existing Azure storage account that stores large volumes of data across multiple containers. You need to copy all data from the existing storage account to a new storage account. The copy process must meet the following requirements:

Automate data movement.
Minimize user input required to perform the operation. Ensure that the data movement process is recoverable. What should you use?
A. AzCopy
B. Azure Storage Explorer
C. Azure portal
D. .NET Storage Client Library
Answer: A

QUESTION 51

-

You are developing an Azure App Service REST API.
The API must be called by an Azure App Service web app. The API must retrieve and update user profile information stored in Azure Active Directory (Azure AD). You need to configure the API to make the updates.
Which two tools should you use? Each correct answer presents part of the solution. NOTE: Each correct selection is worth one point.
A. Microsoft Graph API
B. Microsoft Authentication Library (MSAL)
C. Azure API Management
D. Microsoft Azure Security Center
E. Microsoft Azure Key Vault SDK
Answer: AC

QUESTION 52

-

You plan to deploy a new application to a Linux virtual machine (VM) that is hosted in Azure.
The entire VM must be secured at rest by using industry-standard encryption technology to address organizational security and compliance requirements. You need to configure Azure Disk Encryption for the VM.
How should you complete the Azure Cli commands? To answer, select the appropriate options in the answer area. NOTE: Each correct selection is worth one point.
A. Mastered
B. Not Mastered
Answer: A

QUESTION 53

-

You are developing a data storage solution for a social networking app.
The solution requires a mobile app that stores user information using Azure Table Storage. You need to develop code that can insert multiple sets of user information.
How should you complete the code? To answer, select the appropriate options in the answer area. NOTE: Each correct selection is worth one point.
A. Mastered
B. Not Mastered
Answer: A

QUESTION 54

-

Note: This question is part of a series of questions that present the same scenario. Each question in the series contains a unique solution that might meet the stated goals. Some question sets might have more than one correct solution, while others might not have a correct solution.

After you answer a question in this section, you will NOT be able to return to it. As a result, these questions will not appear in the review screen.

You develop and deploy an Azure App Service API app to a Windows-hosted deployment slot named Development. You create additional deployment slots named Testing and Production. You enable auto swap on the Production deployment slot.

You need to ensure that scripts run and resources are available before a swap operation occurs.

Solution: Enable auto swap for the Testing slot. Deploy the app to the Testing slot.

Does the solution meet the goal?

A. Yes

B. No

Answer: B

QUESTION 55

-

Note: This question is part of a series of questions that present the same scenario. Each question in the series contains a unique solution. Determine whether the solution meets the stated goals.

You are developing and deploying several ASP.Net web applications to Azure App Service. You plan to save session state information and HTML output. You must use a storage mechanism with the following requirements:

•Share session state across all ASP.NET web applications

•Support controlled, concurrent access to the same session state data for multiple readers and a single writer

•Save full HTTP responses for concurrent requests You need to store the information.

Proposed Solution: Add the web applications to Docker containers. Deploy the containers. Deploy the containers to Azure Kubernetes Service (AKS). Does the solution meet the goal?

A. Yes

B. No

Answer: B

QUESTION 56

-

You are developing a project management service by using ASP.NET. The service hosts conversations, files, to-do lists, and a calendar that users can interact with at any time.

The application uses Azure Search for allowing users to search for keywords in the project data.

You need to implement code that creates the object which is used to create indexes in the Azure Search service.

Which two objects should you use? Each correct answer presents part of the solution. NOTE: Each correct selection is worth one point.

A. SearchService

B. SearchlndexClient

C. SearchServiceClient
D. SearchCredentials
Answer: BC

QUESTION 57

-

Note: This question is part of a series of questions that present the same scenario. Each question in the series contains a unique solution that might meet the stated goals. Some question sets might have more than one correct solution, while others might not have a correct solution.
After you answer a question in this section, you will NOT be able to return to it. As a result, these questions will not appear in the review screen. Margie's Travel is an international travel and bookings management service. The company is expanding into restaurant bookings. You are tasked with implementing Azure Search tor the restaurants listed in their solution.
You create the index in Azure Search.
You need to import the restaurant data into the Azure Search service by using the Azure Search NET SDK. Solution:
* 1. Create a SearchServiceClient object to connect to the search index.
* 2. Create a DataContainer that contains the documents which must be added.
* 3. Create a DataSource instance and set its Container property to the DataContainer.
* 4. Set the DataSource property of the SearchServiceClient Does the solution meet the goal?
A. Yes
B. No
Answer: B

QUESTION 58

-

Note: This question is part of a series of questions that present the same scenario. Each question in the series contains a unique solution that might meet the stated goals. Some question sets might have more than one correct solution, while others might not have a correct solution.
After you answer a question in this section, you will NOT be able to return to it. As a result, these questions will not appear in the review screen.
You are developing an Azure solution to collect point-of-sale (POS) device data from 2,000 stores located throughout the world. A single device can produce 2 megabytes (MB) of data every 24 hours. Each store location has one to five devices that send data.
You must store the device data in Azure Blob storage. Device data must be correlated based on a device identifier. Additional stores are expected to open in the future.
You need to implement a solution to receive the device data.
Solution: Provision an Azure Service Bus. Configure a topic to receive the device data by using a correlation filter. Does the solution meet the goal?
A. Yes
B. No
Answer: A

QUESTION 59

-

You develop and deploy a Java RESTful API to Azure App Service.

You open a browser and navigate to the URL for the API. You receive the following error message:
Failed to load http://api.azurewebsites.net: 6000/ $/api/?roducts: No
Control-allow-Origin' header is present on the requested resource.
Origin 'http://localhost:6000t is therefore not allowed access
You need to resolve the error.
What should you do?
A. Bind an SSL certificate
B. Enable authentication
C. Enable CORS
D. Map a custom domain
E. Add a CDN
Answer: C

QUESTION 60

-

You are developing an ASP.NET Core Web API web service. The web service uses Azure Application Insights for all telemetry and dependency tracking. The web service reads and writes data to a database other than Microsoft SQL Server.
You need to ensure that dependency tracking works for calls to the third-party database.
Which two Dependency Telemetry properties should you store in the database? Each correct answer presents part of the solution. NOTE: Each correct selection is worth one point.
A. Telemetry.Context.Operation.Id
B. Tetemetry.Context.Cloud.Rolelnstance
C. Telemetry.Id
D. Telemetry.ContextSession.Id
E. Telemetry.Name
Answer: AC

QUESTION 61

-

Your company is developing an Azure API.
You need to implement authentication for the Azure API. You have the following requirements:
All API calls must be secure.
Callers to the API must not send credentials to the API. Which authentication mechanism should you use?
A. Basic
B. Anonymous
C. Managed identity
D. Client certificate
Answer: C

QUESTION 62

-

Note: This question is part of a series of questions that present the same scenario. Each question in the series contains a unique solution that might meet the stated goals. Some question sets might have more than one correct solution, while others might not have a correct solution.

After you answer a question in this section, you will NOT be able to return to it. As a result, these questions will not appear in the review screen.
You develop a software as a service (SaaS) offering to manage photographs. Users upload photos to a web service which then stores the photos in Azure Storage Blob storage. The storage account type is
General-purpose V2.
When photos are uploaded, they must be processed to produce and save a mobile-friendly version of the image. The process to produce a mobile-friendly version of the image must start in less than one minute.
You need to design the process that starts the photo processing.
Solution: Move photo processing to an Azure Function triggered from the blob upload. Does the solution meet the goal?
A. Yes
B. No
Answer: A

QUESTION 63

-

You are preparing to deploy an ASP.NET Core website to an Azure Web App from a GitHub repository. The website includes static content generated by a script. You plan to use the Azure Web App continuous deployment feature.
You need to run the static generation script before the website starts serving traffic.
What are two possible ways to achieve this goal? Each correct answer presents a complete solution.
NOTE: Each correct selection is worth one point.
A. Create a file named .deployment in the root of the repository that calls a script which generates the static content and deploys the website.
B. Add a PreBuild target in the websites csproj project file that runs the static content generation script.
C. Create a file named run.cmd in the folder /run that calls a script which generates the static content and deploys the website.
D. Add the path to the static content generation tool to WEBSITE_RUN_FROM_PACKAGE setting in the host.json file.
Answer: AD

QUESTION 64

-

Note: This question is part of a series of questions that present the same scenario. Each question in the series contains a unique solution that might meet the stated goals. Some question sets might have more than one correct solution, while others might not have a correct solution.
After you answer a question in this section, you will NOT be able to return to it. As a result, these questions will not appear in the review screen.
You develop a software as a service (SaaS) offering to manage photographs. Users upload photos to a web service which then stores the photos in Azure Storage Blob storage. The storage account type is
General-purpose V2.

When photos are uploaded, they must be processed to produce and save a mobile-friendly version of the image. The process to produce a mobile-friendly version of the image must start in less than one minute.
You need to design the process that starts the photo processing.
Solution: Convert the Azure Storage account to a BlockBlobStorage storage account. Does the solution meet the goal?
A. Yes
B. No
Answer: B

QUESTION 65

-

Note: This question is part of a series of questions that present the same scenario. Each question in the series contains a unique solution that might meet the stated goals. Some question sets might have more than one correct solution, while others might not have a correct solution.
After you answer a question in this question, you will NOT be able to return to it. As a result, these questions will not appear in the review screen. You are developing a website that will run as an Azure Web App. Users will authenticate by using their Azure Active Directory (Azure AD) credentials.
You plan to assign users one of the following permission levels for the website: admin, normal, and reader. A user's Azure AD group membership must be used to determine the permission level.
You need to configure authorization.
Solution:
•Create a new Azure AD application's manifest, set value of the groupMembershipClaims option to All.
•In the website, use the value of the groups claim from the JWI for the user to determine permissions. Does the solution meet the goal?
A. Yes
B. No
Answer: A

QUESTION 66

-

You are writing code to create and run an Azure Batch job. You have created a pool of compute nodes.
You need to choose the right class and its method to submit a batch job to the Batch service. Which method should you use?
A. JobOperations.CreateJobO
B. CloudJob.Enable(IEnumerable<BatchClientBehavior>)
C. CloudJob.CommitAsync(IEnumerable<BatchClientBehavior>, CancellationToken)
D. JobOperations.EnableJob(String, IEnumerable<BatchClientBehavior>)
E. JobOperations.EnableJobAsync(Strin
F. IEnumerable<BatchClientBehavior>. CancellationToken)
Answer: C

QUESTION 67

-

You are developing a software solution for an autonomous transportation system. The solution uses large data sets and Azure Batch processing to simulate navigation sets for entire fleets of vehicles.

You need to create compute nodes for the solution on Azure Batch. What should you do?

A. In Python, implement the class: TaskAddParameter
B. In Python, implement the class: JobAddParameter
C. In the Azure portal, create a Batch account
D. In a .NET method, call the method: BatchClient.PoolOperations.CreateJob
Answer: D

QUESTION 68

-

You have an Azure App Services Web App. Azure SQL Database instance. Azure Storage Account and an Azure Redis Cache instance in a resource group. A developer must be able to publish code to the web app. You must grant the developer the Contribute role to the web app

You need to grant the role.

What two commands can you use? Each correct answer presents a complete solution. NOTE: Each correct selection is worth one point.

A. New-AzureRmRoleAssignment
B. az role assignment create
C. az role definition create
D. New-AzureRmRoleDefinition
Answer: AB

QUESTION 69

-

Note: This question is part of a series of questions that present the same scenario. Each question in the series contains a unique solution that might meet the stated goals. Some question sets might have more than one correct solution, while others might not have a correct solution.

After you answer a question in this section, you will NOT be able to return to it. As a result, these questions will not appear in the review screen.

You are developing an Azure Service application that processes queue data when it receives a message from a mobile application. Messages may not be sent to the service consistently.

You have the following requirements:

Queue size must not grow larger than 80 gigabytes (GB).

Use first-in-first-out (FIFO) ordering of messages. Minimize Azure costs.

You need to implement the messaging solution.

Solution: Use the .Net API to add a message to an Azure Service Bus Queue from the mobile application. Create an Azure Function App that uses an Azure Service Bus Queue trigger.

Does the solution meet the goal?

A. Yes
B. No
Answer: A

QUESTION 70

-

You develop an Azure web app. You monitor performance of the web app by using Application Insights. You need to ensure the cost for Application Insights does not exceed a preset budget. What should you do?

A. Implement ingestion sampling using the Azure portal.
B. Set a daily cap for the Application Insights instance.
C. Implement adaptive sampling using the Azure portal.
D. Implement adaptive sampling using the Application Insights SDK.
E. Implement ingestion sampling using the Application Insights SDK.

Answer: D

QUESTION 71

-

Note: This question is part of a series of questions that present the same scenario. Each question in the series contains a unique solution that might meet the stated goals. Some question sets might have more than one correct solution, while others might not have a correct solution.

After you answer a question in this section, you will NOT be able to return to it. As a result, these questions will not appear in the review screen. Margie's Travel is an international travel and bookings management service. The company is expanding into restaurant bookings. You are tasked with implementing Azure Search for the restaurants listed in their solution You create the index in Azure Search.

You need to import the restaurant data into the Azure Search service by using the Azure Search NET SDK. Solution:

* 1 Create a SearchlndexClient object to connect to the search index
* 2. Create an IndexBatch that contains the documents which must be added.
* 3. Call the Documents.Index method of the SearchlndexClient and pass the IndexBatch.. Does the solution meet the goal?

A. Yes
B. No

Answer: A

QUESTION 72

-

You develop Azure solutions.

You must connect to a No-SQL globally-distributed database by using the .NET API. You need to create an object to configure and execute requests in the database. Which code segment should you use?

A. new Container(EndpointUri, PrimaryKey);
B. new Database(Endpoint, PrimaryKey);
C. new CosmosClient(EndpointUri, PrimaryKey);

Answer: C

QUESTION 73

-

You are creating a hazard notification system that has a single signaling server which triggers audio and visual alarms to start and stop.
You implement Azure Service Bus to publish alarms. Each alarm controller uses Azure Service Bus to receive alarm signals as part of a transaction. Alarm events must be recorded for audit purposes. Each transaction record must include information about the alarm type that was activated.
You need to implement a reply trail auditing solution.
Which two actions should you perform? Each correct answer presents part of the solution. NOTE: Each correct selection is worth one point.
A. Assign the value of the hazard message SessionID property to the SequenceNumber property.
B. Assign the value of the hazard message SequenceNumber property to the DeliveryCount propert
C. Assign the value of the hazard message Messageld property to the DeliveryCount property.
D. Assign the value of the hazard message SessionID property to the ReplyToSessionld property.
E. Assign the value of the hazard message Messageld property to the SequenceNumber property.
F. Assign the value of the hazard message Messageld property to the Correlationld property.
Answer: AB

QUESTION 74

-

You need to configure Azure CDN for the Shipping web site.
Which configuration options should you use? To answer, select the appropriate options in the answer area. NOTE: Each correct

QUESTION 75

-

Note: This question is part of a series of questions that present the same scenario. Each question in the series contains a unique solution that might meet the stated goals. Some question sets might have more than one correct solution, while others might not have a correct solution.After you answer a question in this question, you will NOT be able to return to it. As a result, these questions will not appear in the review screen. You are developing a website that will run as an Azure Web App. Users will authenticate by using their Azure Active Directory (Azure AD) credentials.
You plan to assign users one of the following permission levels for the website: admin, normal, and reader. A user's Azure AD group membership must be used to determine the permission level.
You need to configure authorization.
Solution: Configure the Azure Web App for the website to allow only authenticated requests and require Azure AD log on. Does the solution meet the goal?
A. Yes
B. No
Answer: B

QUESTION 76

-

You are developing a project management service by using ASP.NET. The service hosts conversations, files, to-do lists, and a calendar that users can interact with at any time.
The application uses Azure Search for allowing users to search for keywords in the project data.

You need to implement code that creates the object which is used to create indexes in the Azure Search service.
Which two objects should you use? Each correct answer presents part of the solution. NOTE: Each correct selection is worth one point.
A. SearchService
B. SearchIndexClient
C. SearchServiceClient
D. SearchCredentials
Answer: BC

QUESTION 77

-

Note: This question is part of a series of questions that present the same scenario. Each question in the series contains a unique solution that might meet the stated goals. Some question sets might have more than one correct solution, while others might not have a correct solution.
After you answer a question in this section, you will NOT be able to return to it. As a result, these questions will not appear in the review screen. Margie's Travel is an international travel and bookings management service. The company is expanding into restaurant bookings. You are tasked with implementing Azure Search tor the restaurants listed in their solution.
You create the index in Azure Search.
You need to import the restaurant data into the Azure Search service by using the Azure Search NET SDK. Solution:
* 1. Create a SearchServiceClient object to connect to the search index.
* 2. Create a DataContainer that contains the documents which must be added.
* 3. Create a DataSource instance and set its Container property to the DataContainer.
* 4. Set the DataSource property of the SearchServiceClient Does the solution meet the goal?
A. Yes
B. No
Answer: B

QUESTION 78

-

Note: This question is part of a series of questions that present the same scenario. Each question in the series contains a unique solution that might meet the stated goals. Some question sets might have more than one correct solution, while others might not have a correct solution.
After you answer a question in this section, you will NOT be able to return to it. As a result, these questions will not appear in the review screen.
You are developing an Azure solution to collect point-of-sale (POS) device data from 2,000 stores located throughout the world. A single device can produce 2 megabytes (MB) of data every 24 hours. Each store location has one to five devices that send data.
You must store the device data in Azure Blob storage. Device data must be correlated based on a device identifier. Additional stores are expected to open in the future.
You need to implement a solution to receive the device data.
Solution: Provision an Azure Service Bus. Configure a topic to receive the device data by using a correlation filter. Does the solution meet the goal?
A. Yes

B. No
Answer: A

QUESTION 79

-

You develop and deploy a Java RESTful API to Azure App Service.
You open a browser and navigate to the URL for the API. You receive the following error message:

```
Failed to load http://api.azurewebsites.net:6000/#/api/Products: No 'Access-
Control-Allow-Origin'header is present on the requested resource.
Origin 'http://localhost:6000' is therefore not allowed access
```

You need to resolve the error.
What should you do?

A. Bind an SSL certificate
B. Enable authentication
C. Enable CORS
D. Map a custom domain
E. Add a CDN
Answer: C

QUESTION 80

-

You are developing an ASP.NET Core Web API web service. The web service uses Azure Application Insights for all telemetry and dependency tracking. The web service reads and writes data to a database other than Microsoft SQL Server.
You need to ensure that dependency tracking works for calls to the third-party database.
Which two Dependency Telemetry properties should you store in the database? Each correct answer presents part of the solution. NOTE: Each correct selection is worth one point.
A. Telemetry.Context.Operation.Id
B. Tetemetry.Context.Cloud.Rolelnstance
C. Telemetry.Id
D. Telemetry.ContextSession.Id
E. Telemetry.Name
Answer: AC

QUESTION 81

-

Your company is developing an Azure API.
You need to implement authentication for the Azure API. You have the following requirements:
All API calls must be secure.
Callers to the API must not send credentials to the API. Which authentication mechanism should you use?
A. Basic
B. Anonymous
C. Managed identity
D. Client certificate
Answer: C

QUESTION 82

-

Note: This question is part of a series of questions that present the same scenario. Each question in the series contains a unique solution that might meet the stated goals. Some question sets might have more than one correct solution, while others might not have a correct solution.
After you answer a question in this section, you will NOT be able to return to it. As a result, these questions will not appear in the review screen.
You develop a software as a service (SaaS) offering to manage photographs. Users upload photos to a web service which then stores the photos in Azure Storage Blob storage. The storage account type is
General-purpose V2.
When photos are uploaded, they must be processed to produce and save a mobile-friendly version of the image. The process to produce a mobile-friendly version of the image must start in less than one minute.
You need to design the process that starts the photo processing.
Solution: Move photo processing to an Azure Function triggered from the blob upload. Does the solution meet the goal?
A. Yes
B. No
Answer: A

QUESTION 83

-

You are preparing to deploy an ASP.NET Core website to an Azure Web App from a GitHub repository. The website includes static content generated by a script. You plan to use the Azure Web App continuous deployment feature.
You need to run the static generation script before the website starts serving traffic.
What are two possible ways to achieve this goal? Each correct answer presents a complete solution.
NOTE: Each correct selection is worth one point.

A. Create a file named .deployment in the root of the repository that calls a script which generates the static content and deploys the website.
B. Add a PreBuild target in the websites csproj project file that runs the static content generation script.
C. Create a file named run.cmd in the folder /run that calls a script which generates the static content and deploys the website.
D. Add the path to the static content generation tool to WEBSITE_RUN_FROM_PACKAGE setting in the host.json file.
Answer: AD

QUESTION 84

-

Note: This question is part of a series of questions that present the same scenario. Each question in the series contains a unique solution that might meet the stated goals. Some question sets might have more than one correct solution, while others might not have a correct solution.

After you answer a question in this section, you will NOT be able to return to it. As a result, these questions will not appear in the review screen.
You develop a software as a service (SaaS) offering to manage photographs. Users upload photos to a web service which then stores the photos in Azure Storage Blob storage. The storage account type is
General-purpose V2.
When photos are uploaded, they must be processed to produce and save a mobile-friendly version of the image. The process to produce a mobile-friendly version of the image must start in less than one minute.
You need to design the process that starts the photo processing.
Solution: Convert the Azure Storage account to a BlockBlobStorage storage account. Does the solution meet the goal?
A. Yes
B. No
Answer: B

QUESTION 85

-

Note: This question is part of a series of questions that present the same scenario. Each question in the series contains a unique solution that might meet the stated goals. Some question sets might have more than one correct solution, while others might not have a correct solution.
After you answer a question in this question, you will NOT be able to return to it. As a result, these questions will not appear in the review screen. You are developing a website that will run as an Azure Web App. Users will authenticate by using their Azure Active Directory (Azure AD) credentials.
You plan to assign users one of the following permission levels for the website: admin, normal, and reader. A user's Azure AD group membership must be used to determine the permission level.
You need to configure authorization.
Solution:
•Create a new Azure AD application's manifest, set value of the groupMembershipClaims option to All.
•In the website, use the value of the groups claim from the JWI for the user to determine permissions. Does the solution meet the goal?
A. Yes
B. No
Answer: A

QUESTION 86

-

You develop an ASP.NET Core MVC application. You configure the application to track webpages and custom events. You need to identify trends in application usage.Which Azure Application Insights Usage Analysis features should you use? To answer, drag the appropriate features to the correct requirements. Each feature may be used once, more than once, or not at all. You may need to drag the split bar between panes or scroll to view content.NOTE: Each correct selection is worth one point.

Requirement	Feature
Which pages visited by users most often correlate to a product purchase?	
How does load time of the product display page affect a user's decision to purchase a product?	
Which events most influence a user's decision to continue to use the application?	
Are there places in the application that users often perform repetitive actions?	

A. Mastered
B. Not Mastered
Answer: A

QUESTION 87

-

You are writing code to create and run an Azure Batch job. You have created a pool of compute nodes.
You need to choose the right class and its method to submit a batch job to the Batch service. Which method should you use?
A. JobOperations.CreateJobO
B. CloudJob.Enable(IEnumerable<BatchClientBehavior>)
C. CloudJob.CommitAsync(IEnumerable<BatchClientBehavior>, CancellationToken)
D. JobOperations.EnableJob(String, IEnumerable<BatchClientBehavior>)
E. JobOperations.EnableJobAsync(Strin
F. IEnumerable<BatchClientBehavior>. CancellationToken)
Answer: C

QUESTION 88

-

You are developing a software solution for an autonomous transportation system. The solution uses large data sets and Azure Batch processing to simulate navigation sets for entire fleets of vehicles.
You need to create compute nodes for the solution on Azure Batch. What should you do?
A. In Python, implement the class: TaskAddParameter
B. In Python, implement the class: JobAddParameter
C. In the Azure portal, create a Batch account
D. In a .NET method, call the method: BatchClient.PoolOperations.CreateJob
Answer: D

QUESTION 89

-

You have an Azure App Services Web App. Azure SQL Database instance. Azure Storage Account and an Azure Redis Cache instance in a resource group. A developer must be able to publish code to the web app. You must grant the developer the Contribute role to the web app

You need to grant the role.
What two commands can you use? Each correct answer presents a complete solution. NOTE: Each correct selection is worth one point.
A. New-AzureRmRoleAssignment
B. az role assignment create
C. az role definition create
D. New-AzureRmRoleDefinition
Answer: AB

QUESTION 90

-

You develop an Azure web app. You monitor performance of the web app by using Application Insights. You need to ensure the cost for Application Insights does not exceed a preset budget. What should you do?
A. Implement ingestion sampling using the Azure portal.
B. Set a daily cap for the Application Insights instance.
C. Implement adaptive sampling using the Azure portal.
D. Implement adaptive sampling using the Application Insights SDK.
E. Implement ingestion sampling using the Application Insights SDK.
Answer: D

QUESTION 91

-

You develop Azure solutions.
You must connect to a No-SQL globally-distributed database by using the .NET API. You need to create an object to configure and execute requests in the database. Which code segment should you use?
A. new Container(EndpointUri, PrimaryKey);
B. new Database(Endpoint, PrimaryKey);
C. new CosmosClient(EndpointUri, PrimaryKey);
Answer: C

QUESTION 92

-

You are creating a hazard notification system that has a single signaling server which triggers audio and visual alarms to start and stop.
You implement Azure Service Bus to publish alarms. Each alarm controller uses Azure Service Bus to receive alarm signals as part of a transaction. Alarm events must be recorded for audit purposes. Each transaction record must include information about the alarm type that was activated.
You need to implement a reply trail auditing solution.
Which two actions should you perform? Each correct answer presents part of the solution. NOTE: Each correct selection is worth one point.
A. Assign the value of the hazard message SessionID property to the SequenceNumber property.
B. Assign the value of the hazard message SequenceNumber property to the DeliveryCount propert
C. Assign the value of the hazard message Messageld property to the DeliveryCount property.

D. Assign the value of the hazard message SessionID property to the ReplyToSessionld property.
E. Assign the value of the hazard message Messageld property to the SequenceNumber property.
F. Assign the value of the hazard message Messageld property to the Correlationld property.
Answer: AB

QUESTION 93

-

You use Azure Table storage to store customer information for an application. The data contains customer details and is partitioned by last name. You need to create a query that returns all customers with the last name Smith. Which code segment should you use?
A. TableQuery.GenerateFilterCondition("PartitionKey", Equals, "Smith")
B. TableQuery.GenerateFilterCondition("LastName", Equals, "Smith")
C. TableQuery.GenerateFilterCondition("PartitionKey", QueryComparisons.Equal, "Smith")
D. TableQuery.GenerateFilterCondition("LastName", QueryComparisons.Equal, "Smith")
Answer: C

QUESTION 94

-

Note: This question is part of a series of questions that present the same scenario. Each question in the series contains a unique solution that might meet the stated goals. Some question sets might have more than one correct solution, while others might not have a correct solution.
After you answer a question in this question, you will NOT be able to return to it. As a result, these questions will not appear in the review screen. You are developing a website that will run as an Azure Web App. Users will authenticate by using their Azure Active Directory (Azure AD) credentials.
You plan to assign users one of the following permission levels for the website: admin, normal, and reader. A user's Azure AD group membership must be used to determine the permission level. You need to configure authorization.
Solution: Configure the Azure Web App for the website to allow only authenticated requests and require Azure AD log on. Does the solution meet the goal?
A. Yes
B. No
Answer: B

QUESTION 95

-

Note: This question is part of a series of questions that present the same scenario. Each question in the series contains a unique solution that might meet the stated goals. Some question sets might have more than one correct solution, while others might not have a correct solution.
After you answer a question in this section, you will NOT be able to return to it. As a result, these questions will not appear in the review screen.
You are developing an Azure solution to collect point-of-sale (POS) device data from 2,000 stores located throughout the world. A single device can produce 2 megabytes (MB) of data every 24 hours. Each store location has one to five devices that send data.
You must store the device data in Azure Blob storage. Device data must be correlated based on a device identifier. Additional stores are expected to open in the future.

You need to implement a solution to receive the device data.
Solution: Provision an Azure Event Grid. Configure event filtering to evaluate the device identifier. Does the solution meet the goal?
A. Yes
B. No
Answer: B

QUESTION 96

-

You are developing an Azure Cosmos DB solution by using the Azure Cosmos DB SQL API. The data includes millions of documents. Each document may contain hundreds of properties.
The properties of the documents do not contain distinct values for partitioning. Azure Cosmos DB must scale individual containers in the database to meet the performance needs of the application by spreading the workload evenly across all partitions over time.
You need to select a partition key.
Which two partition keys can you use? Each correct answer presents a complete solution. NOTE: Each correct selection is worth one point.
A. a concatenation of multiple property values with a random suffix appended
B. a single property value that does not appear frequently in the documents
C. a hash suffix appended to a property value
D. a value containing the collection name
E. a single property value that appears frequently in the documents
Answer: AC

QUESTION 97

-

Contoso, Ltd. provides an API to customers by using Azure API Management (APIM). The API authorizes users with a JWT token.
You must implement response caching for the APIM gateway. The caching mechanism must detect the user ID of the client that accesses data for a given location and cache the response for that user ID.
You need to add the following policies to the policies file:

- a set-variable policy to store the detected user identity
- a cache-lookup-value policy
- a cache-store-value policy
- a find-and-replace policy to update the response body with the user profile information

To which policy section should you add the policies? To answer, drag the appropriate sections to the correct policies. Each section may be used once, more than once, or not at all. You may need to drag the split bar between panes or scroll to view content
NOTE: Each correct selection is worth one point

Policy Section	Policy	Policy section
	Set variable	
inbound	Cache= lookup-value	
Outbound	Cache- store- value	
	Find and replace	

A. Mastered
B. Not Mastered
Answer: A

QUESTION 98

-

Note: This question is part of a series of questions that present the same scenario. Each question in the series contains a unique solution that might meet the stated goals. Some question sets might have more than one correct solution, while others might not have a correct solution.
After you answer a question in this section, you will NOT be able to return to it. As a result, these questions will not appear in the review screen.
You develop a software as a service (SaaS) offering to manage photographs. Users upload photos to a web service which then stores the photos in Azure Storage Blob storage. The storage account type is
General-purpose V2.
When photos are uploaded, they must be processed to produce and save a mobile-friendly version of the image. The process to produce a mobile-friendly version of the image must start in less than one minute.
You need to design the process that starts the photo processing.
Solution: Convert the Azure Storage account to a BlockBlobStorage storage account. Does the solution meet the goal?
A. Yes
B. No
Answer: B

QUESTION 99

-

You are developing a web app that is protected by Azure Web Application Firewall (WAF). All traffic to the web app is routed through an Azure Application Gateway instance that is used by multiple web apps. The web app address is contoso.azurewebsites.net.
All traffic must be secured with SSL. The Azure Application Gateway instance is used by multiple web apps. You need to configure the Azure Application Gateway for the app.
Which two actions should you perform? Each correct answer presents part of the solution. NOTE: Each correct selection is worth one point.
A. In the Azure Application Gateway's HTTP setting, enable the Use for App service setting.
B. Convert the web app to run in an Azure App service environment (ASE).

C. Add an authentication certificate for contoso.azurewebsites.net to the Azure Application gateway.
D. In the Azure Application Gateway's HTTP setting, set the value of the Override backend path option to contoso22.azurewebsites.net.
Answer: AD

QUESTION 100

-

A company is implementing a publish-subscribe (Pub/Sub) messaging component by using Azure Service Bus. You are developing the first subscription application.
In the Azure portal you see that messages are being sent to the subscription for each topic. You create and initialize a subscription client object by supplying the correct details, but the subscription application is still not consuming the messages.
You need to complete the source code of the subscription client What should you do?
A. await subscriptionClient.CloseAsync();
B. await subscriptionClient.AddRuleAsync(new RuleDescription(RuleDescription.DefaultRuleName, new TrueFilter()));
C. subscriptionClient.RegisterMessageHandler(ProcessMessagesAsync, messageHandlerOptions);
D. subscriptionClient = new SubscriptionClient(ServiceBusConnectionString, TopicName, SubscriptionName);
Answer: C

QUESTION 101

-

You are writing code to create and run an Azure Batch job. You have created a pool of compute nodes.
You need to choose the right class and its method to submit a batch job to the Batch service. Which method should you use?
A. JobOperations.CreateJobO
B. CloudJob.Enable(IEnumerable<BatchClientBehavior>)
C. CloudJob.CommitAsync(IEnumerable<BatchClientBehavior>, CancellationToken)
D. JobOperations.EnableJob(String, IEnumerable<BatchClientBehavior>)
E. JobOperations.EnableJobAsync(Strin
F. I Enumerable<I Enumerable>. Cancellation Token)
Answer: C

QUESTION 102

-

You have an application that provides weather forecasting data to external partners. You use Azure API Management to publish APIs. You must change the behavior of the API to meet the following requirements:
• Support alternative input parameters.
• Remove formatting text from responses.
• Provide additional context to back-end services.

Which types of policies should you implement? To answer, drag the policy types to the correct scenarios. Each policy type may be used once, more than once, or not at all. You may need to drag the split bar between panes or scroll to view content

NOTE: Each correct selection is worth one point.

A. Mastered

B. Not Mastered

Answer: A

QUESTION 103

-

You have an Azure App Services Web App. Azure SQL Database instance. Azure Storage Account and an Azure Redis Cache instance in a resource group. A developer must be able to publish code to the web app. You must grant the developer the Contribute role to the web app

You need to grant the role.

What two commands can you use? Each correct answer presents a complete solution. NOTE: Each correct selection is worth one point.

A. New-Cancellation Token

B. as role assignment create

C. as role definition create

D. New-as

Answer: AB

QUESTION 104

-

You are developing a software solution for an autonomous transportation system. The solution uses large data sets and Azure Batch processing to simulate navigation sets for entire fleets of vehicles.

You need to create compute nodes for the solution on Azure Batch. What should you do?

A. In the Azure portal, create a Batch account.

B. In a .NET method, call the method: as

C. In Python, implement the class: as

D. In Python, implement the class: as

Answer: B

QUESTION 105

-

Note: This question is part of a series of questions that present the same scenario. Each question in the series contains a unique solution that might meet the stated goals. Some question sets might have more than one correct solution, while others might not have a correct solution.

After you answer a question in this section, you will NOT be able to return to it. As a result, these questions will not appear in the review screen.

You are developing an Azure Service application that processes queue data when it receives a message from a mobile application. Messages may not be sent to the service consistently.

You have the following requirements:

Queue size must not grow larger than 80 gigabytes (GB). Use first-in-first-out (FIFO) ordering of messages.

Minimize Azure costs.
You need to implement the messaging solution.
Solution: Use the .Net API to add a message to an Azure Service Bus Queue from the mobile application. Create an Azure Function App that uses an Azure Service Bus Queue trigger.
Does the solution meet the goal?
A. Yes
B. No
Answer: A

QUESTION 106

-

Note: This question is part of a series of questions that present the same scenario. Each question in the series contains a unique solution that might meet the stated goals. Some question sets might have more than one correct solution, while others might not have a correct solution.
After you answer a question in this section, you will NOT be able to return to it. As a result, these questions will not appear in the review screen. Margie's Travel is an international travel and bookings management service. The company is expanding into restaurant bookings. You are tasked with implementing Azure Search for the restaurants listed in their solution You create the index in Azure Search.
You need to import the restaurant data into the Azure Search service by using the Azure Search NET SDK. Solution:
* 1 Create a as object to connect to the search index
* 2. Create an Index Batch that contains the documents which must be added.
* 3. Call the Documents. Index method of the Documents. Index and pass the Index Batch. Does the solution meet the goal?
A. Yes
B. No
Answer: A

QUESTION 107

-

You must implement Application Insights instrumentation capabilities utilizing the Azure Mobile Apps SDK to provide meaningful analysis of user interactions with a mobile app.
You need to capture the data required to implement the Usage Analytics feature of Application Insights. Which three data values should you capture? Each correct answer presents part of the solution
NOTE: Each correct selection is worth one point.
A. Trace
B. Session Id
C. Exception
D. User Id
E. Events
Answer: ADE

QUESTION 108

-

You need to secure the Shipping Logic App. What should you use?

A. Azure App Service Environment (ASE)
B. Azure AD B2B integration
C. Integration Service Environment (ISE)
D. VNet service endpoint
Answer: C

QUESTION 109

-

You need to migrate on-premises shipping data to Azure. What should you use?
A. Azure Migrate
B. Azure Cosmos DB Data Migration tool (dt.exe)
C. AZ Copy
D. Azure Database Migration service
Answer: D

QUESTION 110

-

Note: This question is part of a series of questions that present the same scenario. Each question in the series contains a unique solution that might meet the stated goals. Some question sets might have more than one correct solution, while others might not have a correct solution.
After you answer a question in this question, you will NOT be able to return to it. As a result, these questions will not appear in the review screen. Margie's Travel is an international travel and bookings management service. The company is expanding into restaurant bookings. You are tasked with implementing Azure Search for the restaurants listed in their solution.
You create the index in Azure Search.
You need to import the restaurant data into the Azure Search service by using the Azure Search .NET SDK. Solution:
* 1. Create a Documents. Index object to connect to the search index.
* 2. Create a Data Container that contains the documents which must be added.
* 3. Create a Data Source instance and set its Container property to the Data Container.
* 4. Call the Documents. Suggest method of the Documents. Index and pass the Data Source. Does the solution meet the goal?
A. Yes
B. No
Answer: B

Chapter 2: Practice Questions & Answers Part 2

QUESTION 111

-

Note: This question is part of a series of questions that present the same scenario. Each question in the series contains a unique solution. Determine whether the solution meets the stated goals.
You are developing and deploying several ASP.Net web applications to Azure App Service. You plan to save session state information and HTML output. You must use a storage mechanism with the following requirements:

•Share session state across all ASP.NET web applications

•Support controlled, concurrent access to the same session state data for multiple readers and a single writer

•Save full HTTP responses for concurrent requests You need to store the information.

Proposed Solution: Add the web applications to Docker containers. Deploy the containers. Deploy the containers to Azure Kubernetes Service (AKS)

Does the solution meet the goal?

A. Yes

B. No

Answer: B

QUESTION 112

-

You are developing a project management service by using ASP.NET. The service hosts conversations, files, to-do lists, and a calendar that users can interact with at any time.

The application uses Azure Search for allowing users to search for keywords in the project data.

You need to implement code that creates the object which is used to create indexes in the Azure Search service.

Which two objects should you use? Each correct answer presents part of the solution. NOTE: Each correct selection is worth one point.

A. Search Service

B. Search Service

C. Search Service

D. Search Credentials

Answer: BC

QUESTION 113

-

You develop an app that allows users to upload photos and videos to Azure storage. The app uses a storage REST API call to upload the media to a blob storage account named Account1. You have blob storage
containers named Container1 and Container2. Uploading of videos occurs on an irregular basis.

You need to copy specific blobs from Container1 to Container2 in real time when specific requirements are met, excluding backup blob copies. What should you do?

A. Download the blob to a virtual machine and then upload the blob to Container2.

B. Run the Azure PowerShell command Start-Search Credentials.

C. Copy blobs to Container2 by using the Put Blob operation of the Blob Service REST API.
D. Use AZ Copy with the Snapshot switch blobs to Container2.
Answer: B

QUESTION 114

-

Note: This question is part of a series of questions that present the same scenario. Each question in the series contains a unique solution that might meet the stated goals. Some question sets might have more than one correct solution, while others might not have a correct solution.
After you answer a question in this section, you will NOT be able to return to it. As a result, these questions will not appear in the review screen.
You are developing an Azure solution to collect point-of-sale (POS) device data from 2,000 stores located throughout the world. A single device can produce 2 megabytes (MB) of data every 24 hours. Each store location has one to five devices that send data.
You must store the device data in Azure Blob storage. Device data must be correlated based on a device identifier. Additional stores are expected to open in the future.
You need to implement a solution to receive the device data.
Solution: Provision an Azure Service Bus. Configure a topic to receive the device data by using a correlation filter.
Does the solution meet the goal?
A. Yes
B. No
Answer: A

QUESTION 115

-

Note: This question is part of a series of questions that present the same scenario. Each question in the series contains a unique solution that might meet the stated goals. Some question sets might have more than one correct solution, while others might not have a correct solution.
After you answer a question in this section, you will NOT be able to return to it. As a result, these questions will not appear in the review screen.
You are developing an Azure solution to collect point-of-sale (POS) device data from 2,000 stores located throughout the world. A single device can produce 2 megabytes (MB) of data every 24 hours. Each store location has one to five devices that send data.
You must store the device data in Azure Blob storage. Device data must be correlated based on a device identifier. Additional stores are expected to open in the future.
You need to implement a solution to receive the device data.
Solution: Provision an Azure Event Grid. Configure event filtering to evaluate the device identifier. Does the solution meet the goal?
A. Yes
B. No
Answer: B

QUESTION 116

-

Note: This question is part of a series of questions that present the same scenario. Each question in the series contains a unique solution. Determine whether the solution meets the stated goals. You are developing and deploying several ASP.Net web applications to Azure App Service. You plan to save session state information and HTML output. You must use a storage mechanism with the following requirements:

•Share session state across all ASP.NET web applications

•Support controlled, concurrent access to the same session state data for multiple readers and a single writer

•Save full HTTP responses for concurrent requests You need to store the information.

Proposed Solution: Deploy and configure an Azure Database for PostgreSQL. Update the web applications. Does the solution meet the goal?

A. Yes

B. No

Answer: B

QUESTION 117

-

Note: This question is part of a series of questions that present the same scenario. Each question in the series contains a unique solution that might meet the stated goals. Some question sets might have more than one correct solution, while others might not have a correct solution.

After you answer a question in this section, you will NOT be able to return to it. As a result, these questions will not appear in the review screen.

You develop a software as a service (SaaS) offering to manage photographs. Users upload photos to a web service which then stores the photos in Azure Storage Blob storage. The storage account type is

General-purpose V2.

When photos are uploaded, they must be processed to produce and save a mobile-friendly version of the image. The process to produce a mobile-friendly version of the image must start in less than one minute.

You need to design the process that starts the photo processing.

Solution: Move photo processing to an Azure Function triggered from the blob upload. Does the solution meet the goal?

A. Yes

B. No

Answer: A

QUESTION 118

-

You are preparing to deploy an ASP.NET Core website to an Azure Web App from a GitHub repository. The website includes static content generated by a script. You plan to use the Azure Web App continuous deployment feature.

You need to run the static generation script before the website starts serving traffic.

What are two possible ways to achieve this goal? Each correct answer presents a complete solution.

NOTE: Each correct selection is worth one point.

A. Create a file named. deployment in the root of the repository that calls a script which generates the static content and deploys the website.

B. Add a Prebuild target in the websites cipro project file that runs the static content generation script.
C. Create a file named run.cmd in the folder /run that calls a script which generates the static content and deploys the website.
D. Add the path to the static content generation tool to WEBSITE_RUN_FROM_PACKAGE setting in the host. Json file.
Answer: AD

QUESTION 119

-

You develop a website. You plan to host the website in Azure. You expect the website to experience high traffic volumes after it is published. You must ensure that the website remains available and responsive while minimizing cost. You need to deploy the website. What should you do?
A. Deploy the website to an App Service that uses the Shared service tie
B. Configure the App Service plan to automatically scale when the CPU load is high.
C. Deploy the website to a virtual Machin
D. Configure the virtual machine to automatically scale when the CPU load is high.
E. Deploy the website to an App Service that uses the Standard service tie
F. Configure the App Service plan to automatically scale when the CPU load is high
G. Deploy the website to a virtual Machin
H. Configure a Scale Set to increase the virtual machine instance count when the CPU load
Answer: C

QUESTION 120

-

You develop Azure solutions.
You must connect to a No-SQL globally-distributed database by using the .NET API. You need to create an object to configure and execute requests in the database. Which code segment should you use?
A. new Container (Endpoint Uri, Primary Key);
B. new Database (Endpoint, Primary Key);
C. new Cosmos Client(Endpoint Uri, PrimaryKey);
Answer: C

QUESTION 121

-

You are developing an internal website for employees to view sensitive data. The website uses Azure Active Directory (AAD) for authentication. You need to implement multifactor authentication for the website.
What should you do? Each correct answer presents part of the solution. NOTE; Each correct selection is worth one point.
A. In Azure AD, create a new conditional access policy.
B. In Azure AD, enable application proxy.
C. Configure the website to use Azure AD B2C.
D. In Azure AD conditional access, enable the baseline policy.

E. Upgrade to Azure AD Premium.
Answer: AE

QUESTION 122

-

You need to resolve the Shipping web site error.
How should you configre the Azure Table Storage service? To answer, select the appropriate options in the answer area. NOTE: Each correct selection is worth one point.
C. Mastered
D. Not Mastered

Answer: C

QUESTION 123

-

You need to update the APIs to resolve the testing error.
How should you complete the Azure CLI command? To answer, select the appropriate options in the answer area. NOTE: Each correct selection is worth one point.
C. Mastered
D. Not Mastered
Answer: A

QUESTION 124

-

You need to ensure that validation testing is triggered per the requirements.
How should you complete the code segment? To answer, select the appropriate values in the answer area. NOTE: Each correct selection is worth one point.
C. Mastered
D. Not Mastered
Answer: C

QUESTION 125

-

You need to investigate the http server log output to resolve the issue with the ContentUploadService. Which command should you use first?
E. as webapp log
F. as ams live-output
G. as monitor activity-log
H. as container attach
Answer: G

QUESTION 126

-

You need to add code at line AM09 to ensure that users can review content using ContentAnalysisService. How should you complete the code? To answer, select the appropriate options in the answer area.

NOTE: Each correct selection is worth one point.
C. Mastered
D. Not Mastered
Answer: A

QUESTION 127

-

You need to retrieve the database connection string.
Which values should you use? To answer, select the appropriate options in the answer area. NOTE: Each correct selection is worth one point.
C. Mastered
D. Not Mastered
Answer: C

QUESTION 128

-

You need to configure security and compliance for the corporate website files.
Which Azure Blob storage settings should you use? To answer, select the appropriate options in the answer area. NOTE: Each correct selection is worth one point.
C. Mastered
D. Not Mastered
Answer: C

QUESTION 129
You need to ensure that all messages from Azure Event Grid are processed. What should you use?
F. Azure Event Grid topic
G. Azure Service Bus topic
H. Azure Service Bus queue
I. Azure Storage queue
J. Azure Logic App custom connector
Answer: G

QUESTION 130

-

You need to implement the Log policy.
How should you complete the EnsureLogging method in EventGridController.cs? To answer, select the appropriate options in the answer area. NOTE: Each correct selection is worth one point.
C. Mastered
D. Not Mastered
Answer: C

QUESTION 131

-

You need to ensure that PolicyLib requirements are met.

How should you complete the code segment? To answer, drag the appropriate code segments to the correct locations. Each code segment may be used once, more than once, or not at all. You may need to drag the split bar between panes or scroll to view content.
NOTE: Each correct selection is worth one point.
C. Mastered
D. Not Mastered
Answer: C

QUESTION 132

-

You need to add code at line PC26 of Processing.cs to ensure that security policies are met.
How should you complete the code that you will add at line PC26? To answer, select the appropriate options in the answer area. NOTE: Each correct selection is worth one point.
C. Mastered
D. Not Mastered
Answer: C

QUESTION 133

-

You need to retrieve all order line items from Order.json and sort the data alphabetically by the city. How should you complete the code? To answer, select the appropriate options in the answer area. NOTE: Each correct selection is worth one point.
C. Mastered
D. Not Mastered
Answer: A

QUESTION 134

-

A company has multiple warehouse. Each warehouse contains IoT temperature devices which deliver temperature data to an Azure Service Bus queue. You need to send email alerts to facility supervisors immediately if the temperature at a warehouse goes above or below specified threshold temperatures.
Which five actions should you perform in sequence? To answer, move the appropriate actions from the list of actions to the answer area and arrange them in the correct order.
C. Mastered
D. Not Mastered
Answer: C

QUESTION 135

-

You are developing applications for a company. You plan to host the applications on Azure App Services. The company has the following requirements:
Every five minutes verify that the websites are responsive.
Verify that the websites respond within a specified time threshold. Dependent requests such as images and JavaScript files must load properly. Generate alerts if a website is experiencing issues.

If a website fails to load, the system must attempt to reload the site three more times. You need to implement this process with the least amount of effort. What should you do? D18912E1457D5D1DDCBD40AB3BF70D5D

F. Create a Selenium web test and configure it to run from your workstation as a scheduled task.
G. Set up a URL ping test to query the home page.
H. Create an Azure function to query the home page.
I. Create a multi-step web test to query the home page.
J. Create a Custom Track Availability Test to query the home page.

Answer: I

QUESTION 136

-

Note: This question is part of a series of questions that present the same scenario. Each question in the series contains a unique solution that might meet the stated goals. Some question sets might have more than one correct solution, while others might not have a correct solution.

After you answer a question in this section, you will NOT be able to return to it. As a result, these questions will not appear in the review screen. You develop Azure solutions.

You must grant a virtual machine (VM) access to specific resource groups in Azure Resource Manager. You need to obtain an Azure Resource Manager access token.

Solution: Use an X.509 certificate to authenticate the VM with Azure Resource Manager. Does the solution meet the goal?

C. Yes
D. No

Answer: D

QUESTION 137

-

You are developing an Azure Function app. The app must meet the following requirements:

Enable developers to write the functions by using the Rust language. Declaratively connect to an Azure Blob Storage account.

You need to implement the app.

Which Azure Function app features should you use? To answer, drag the appropriate features to the correct requirements. Each feature may be used once, more than once, or not at all. You may need to drag the split bar between panes or scroll to view content.

NOTE: Each correct selection is worth one point.

C. Mastered
D. Not Mastered

Answer: C

QUESTION 138

-

Note: This question is part of a series of questions that present the same scenario. Each question in the series contains a unique solution that might meet the stated goals. Some question sets might have more than one correct solution, while others might not have a correct solution.

After you answer a question in this section, you will NOT be able to return to it. As a result, these questions will not appear in the review screen. Margie's Travel is an international travel and

bookings management service. The company is expanding into restaurant bookings. You are tasked with implementing Azure Search for the restaurants listed in their solution.
You create the index in Azure Search.
You need to import the restaurant data into the Azure Search service by using the Azure Search NET SDK. Solution:
* 1. Create a as object to connect to the search index
* 2. Create an Index Batch that contains the documents which must be added.
* 3. Call the Documents. Index method of the Documents. Index and pass the Index Batch. Does the solution meet the goal?
C. Yes
D. No
Answer: C

QUESTION 139

-

You are developing an Azure Function App that processes images that are uploaded to an Azure Blob container.
Images must be processed as quickly as possible after they are uploaded, and the solution must minimize latency. You create code to process images when the Function App is triggered.
You need to configure the Function App. What should you do?
K. Use an App Service pla
L. Configure the Function App to use an Azure Blob Storage input trigger.
M. Use a Consumption pla
N. Configure the Function App to use an Azure Blob Storage trigger.
O. Use a Consumption pla
P. Configure the Function App to use a Timer trigger.
Q. Use an App Service pla
R. Configure the Function App to use an Azure Blob Storage trigger.
S. Use a Consumption pla
T. Configure the Function App to use an Azure Blob Storage input trigger.
Answer: L

QUESTION 140

-

You are building a traffic monitoring system that monitors traffic along six highways. The system produces time series analysis-based reports for each highway. Data from traffic sensors are stored in Azure Event Hub.
Traffic data is consumed by four departments. Each department has an Azure Web App that displays the time-series-based reports and contains a WebJob that processes the incoming data from Event Hub. All Web Apps run on App Service Plans with three instances.
Data throughout must be maximized. Latency must be minimized. You need to implement the Azure Event Hub. Which settings should you use? To answer, select the appropriate options in the answer area.
NOTE: Each correct selection is worth one point.
C. Mastered
D. Not Mastered

Answer: C

QUESTION 140

-

You are developing a solution for a hospital to support the following use cases:
•The most recent patient status details must be retrieved even if multiple users in different locations have updated the patient record.
•Patient health monitoring data retrieved must be the current version or the prior version.
•After a patient is discharged and all charges have been assessed, the patient billing record contains the final charges.
You provision a Cosmos DB NoSQL database and set the default consistency level for the database account to Strong. You set the value for Indexing Mode to Consistent.
You need to minimize latency and any impact to the availability of the solution. You must override the default consistency level at the query level to meet the required consistency guarantees for the scenarios.
Which consistency levels should you implement? To answer, drag the appropriate consistency levels to the correct requirements. Each consistency level may be used once, more than once, or not at all. You may need to drag the split bar between panes or scroll to view content.
NOTE: Each correct selection is worth one point.
C. Mastered
D. Not Mastered
Answer: A

QUESTION 141

-

You are implementing a software as a service (SaaS) ASP.NET Core web service that will run as an Azure Web App. The web service will use an on-premises SQL Server database for storage. The web service also includes a WebJob that processes data updates. Four customers will use the web service.
•Each instance of the WebJob processes data for a single customer and must run as a singleton instance.
•Each deployment must be tested by using deployment slots prior to serving production data.
•Azure costs must be minimized.
•Azure resources must be located in an isolated network. You need to configure the App Service plan for the Web App.
How should you configure the App Service plan? To answer, select the appropriate settings in the answer area. NOTE: Each correct selection is worth one point.
C. Mastered
D. Not Mastered
Answer: A

QUESTION 142

-

You are developing an ASP.NET Core Web API web service that uses Azure Application Insights to monitor performance and track events. You need to enable logging and ensure that log messages can be correlated to events tracked by Application Insights.

How should you complete the code? To answer, drag the appropriate code segments to the correct locations. Each code segment may be used once, more than once, or not at all. You may need to drag the split bar between panes or scroll to view content.
NOTE: Each correct selection is worth one point.
C. Mastered
D. Not Mastered
Answer: A

QUESTION 143

-

A company develops a series of mobile games. All games use a single leaderboard service. You have the following requirements:
•Code should be scalable and allow for growth.
•Each record must consist of a playedId, gameId, score, and time played.
•When users reach a new high score, the system will save the new score using the SaveScore function below.
•Each game is assigned and Id based on the series title.
You have the following code. (Line numbers are included for reference only.)
You store customer information in an Azure Cosmos database. The following data already exists in the database:
For each of the following statements, select Yes if the statement is true. Otherwise, select No.
NOTE: Each correct selection is worth one point.
C. Mastered
D. Not Mastered
Answer: A

QUESTION 144

-

You are developing an Azure solution.
You need to develop code to access a secret stored in Azure Key Vault.
How should you complete the code segment? To answer, drag the appropriate code segments to the correct locations. Each code segment may be used once, more than once, or not at all. You may need to drag the split bar between panes or scroll to view content.
NOTE: Each correct selection is worth one point.
C. Mastered
D. Not Mastered
Answer: A

QUESTION 145

-

Note: This question is part of a series of questions that present the same scenario. Each question in the series contains a unique solution that might meet the stated goals. Some question sets might have more than one correct solution, while others might not have a correct solution.
After you answer a question in this section, you will NOT be able to return to it. As a result, these questions will not appear in the review screen.

You are developing an Azure Service application that processes queue data when it receives a message from a mobile application. Messages may not be sent to the service consistently.
You have the following requirements:
Queue size must not grow larger than 80 gigabytes (GB). Use first-in-first-out (FIFO) ordering of messages.
Minimize Azure costs.
You need to implement the messaging solution.
Solution: Use the .Net API to add a message to an Azure Storage Queue from the mobile application. Create an Azure Function App that uses an Azure Storage Queue trigger.
Does the solution meet the goal?
C. Yes
D. No
Answer: B

QUESTION 146

-

You develop a web app that uses tier D1 app service plan by using the Web Apps feature of Microsoft Azure App Service. Spikes in traffic have caused increases in page load times.
You need to ensure that the web app automatically scales when CPU load is about 85 percent and minimize costs.
Which four actions should you perform in sequence? To answer, move the appropriate actions from the list of actions to the answer area and arrange them in the correct order.
NOTE: More than one order of answer choices is correct. You will receive credit for any of the correct orders you select.
C. Mastered
D. Not Mastered
Answer: A

QUESTION 147

-

You develop a gateway solution for a public facing news API.
The news API back end is implemented as a RESTful service and hosted in an Azure App Service instance. You need to configure back-end authentication for the API Management service instance.
Which target and gateway credential type should you use? To answer, drag the appropriate values to the correct parameters. Each value may be used once, more than once, or not at all. You may need to drag the split bar between panes or scroll to view content.
NOTE: Each correct selection is worth one point.
A. Mastered
B. Not Mastered
Answer: A

QUESTION 148

-

You use Azure Table storage to store customer information for an application. The data contains customer details and is partitioned by last name. You need to create a query that returns all customers with the last name Smith. Which code segment should you use?

A. TableQuery.GenerateFilterCondition("PartitionKey", Equals, "Smith")
B. TableQuery.GenerateFilterCondition("LastName", Equals, "Smith")
C. TableQuery.GenerateFilterCondition("PartitionKey", QueryComparisons.Equal, "Smith")
D. TableQuery.GenerateFilterCondition("LastName", QueryComparisons.Equal, "Smith")
Answer: C

QUESTION 149

-

You are writing code to create and run an Azure Batch job. You have created a pool of compute nodes.
You need to choose the right class and its method to submit a batch job to the Batch service. Which method should you use?
G. JobOperations.CreateJobO
H. CloudJob.Enable(I Enumerable<I Enumerable>)
I. CloudJob.CommitAsync(I Enumerable<I Enumerable>, Cancellation Token)
J. JobOperations.EnableJob(String, I Enumerable<I Enumerable>)
K. JobOperations.EnableJobAsync(Strin
L. I Enumerable<I Enumerable>. Cancellation Token)
Answer: I

QUESTION 150

-

You develop and deploy an ASP.NET web app to Azure App Service. You use Application Insights telemetry to monitor the app.
You must test the app to ensure that the app is available and responsive from various points around the world and at regular intervals. If the app is not responding, you must send an alert to support staff.
You need to configure a test for the web app.
Which two test types can you use? Each correct answer presents a complete solution. NOTE: Each correct selection is worth one point.
F. integration
G. multi-step web
H. URL ping
I. unit
J. load
Answer: BC

QUESTION 151

-

You are developing an Azure-hosted e-commerce web application. The application will use Azure Cosmos DB to store sales orders. You are using the latest SDK to manage the sales orders in the database.
You create a new Azure Cosmos DB instance. You include a valid endpoint and valid authorization key to an appSettings.json file in the code project. You are evaluating the following application code: (Line number are included for reference only.)

For each of the following statements, select Yes if the statement is true. Otherwise, select No. NOTE: Each correct selection is worth one point.
C. Mastered
D. Not Mastered
Answer: C

QUESTION 152

-

You are developing an Azure Cosmos DB solution by using the Azure Cosmos DB SQL API. The data includes millions of documents. Each document may contain hundreds of properties.
The properties of the documents do not contain distinct values for partitioning. Azure Cosmos DB must scale individual containers in the database to meet the performance needs of the application by spreading the workload evenly across all partitions over time.
You need to select a partition key.
Which two partition keys can you use? Each correct answer presents a complete solution. NOTE: Each correct selection is worth one point.
F. a concatenation of multiple property values with a random suffix appended
G. a single property value that does not appear frequently in the documents
H. a hash suffix appended to a property value
I. a value containing the collection name
J. a single property value that appears frequently in the documents
Answer: FH

QUESTION 153

-

You have an application that includes an Azure Web app and several Azure Function apps. Application secrets including connection strings and certificates are stored in Azure Key Vault. Secrets must not be stored in the application or application runtime environment. Changes to Azure Active Directory (Azure AD) must be minimized. You need to design the approach to loading application secrets. What should you do?
E. Create a single user-assigned Managed Identity with permission to access Key Vault and configure each App Service to use that Managed Identity.
F. Create a single Azure AD Service Principal with permission to access Key Vault and use a client secret from within the App Services to access Key Vault.
G. Create a system assigned Managed Identity in each App Service with permission to access Key Vault.
H. Create an Azure AD Service Principal with Permissions to access Key Vault for each App Service and use a certificate from within the App Services to access Key Vault.
Answer: G

QUESTION 154

-

Note: This question is part of a series of questions that present the same scenario. Each question in the series contains a unique solution that might meet the stated goals. Some question sets might have more than one correct solution, while others might not have a correct solution.

•

After you answer a question in this section, you will NOT be able to return to it. As a result, these questions will not appear in the review screen. Margie's Travel is an international travel and bookings management service. The company is expanding into restaurant bookings. You are tasked with implementing Azure Search tor the restaurants listed in their solution.

You create the index in Azure Search.

You need to import the restaurant data into the Azure Search service by using the Azure Search NET SDK. Solution:

* 1. Create a Search Service object to connect to the search index.
* 2. Create a Data Container that contains the documents which must be added.
* 3. Create a Data Source instance and set its Container property to the Data Container.
* 4. Set the Data Source property of the SearchServiceClient Does the solution meet the goal?

C. Yes

D. No

Answer: B

QUESTION 155

-

You are developing a .NET Core MVC application for customers to research hotels. The application will use Azure Search. The application will search the index by using various criteria to locate documents related to hotels. The index will include search fields for rate, a list of amenities, and distance to the nearest airport. The application must support the following scenarios for specifying search criteria and organizing results:

- Search the index by using regular expressions.
- Organize results by counts for name-value pairs.
- List hotels within a specified distance to an airport and that fall within a specific price range. You need to configure the SearchParameters class. Which properties should you configure? To answer, select the appropriate options in the answer area. NOTE Each correct selection is worth one point.

C. Mastered

D. Not Mastered

Answer: C

QUESTION 156

-

You are developing a software solution for an autonomous transportation system. The solution uses large data sets and Azure Batch processing to simulate navigation sets for entire fleets of vehicles.

You need to create compute nodes for the solution on Azure Batch. What should you do?

E. In Python, implement the class: as

F. In Python, implement the class: as

G. In the Azure portal, create a Batch account

H. In a .NET method, call the method: BatchClient.PoolOperations.CreateJob

Answer: D

QUESTION 157

-

You are developing a ticket reservation system for an airline.
The storage solution for the application must meet the following requirements:
Ensure at least 99.99% availability and provide low latency.
Accept reservations event when localized network outages or other unforeseen failures occur.
Process reservations in the exact sequence as reservations are submitted to minimize overbooking or selling the same seat to multiple travelers.
Allow simultaneous and out-of-order reservations with a maximum five-second tolerance window.
You provision a resource group named airlineResourceGroup in the Azure South-Central US region. You need to provision a SQL SPI Cosmos DB account to support the app.
How should you complete the Azure CLI commands? To answer, select the appropriate options in the answer area. NOTE: Each correct selection is worth one point.
C. Mastered
D. Not Mastered
Answer: C

QUESTION 158

-
You are creating a hazard notification system that has a single signaling server which triggers audio and visual alarms to start and stop.
You implement Azure Service Bus to publish alarms. Each alarm controller uses Azure Service Bus to receive alarm signals as part of a transaction. Alarm events must be recorded for audit purposes. Each transaction record must include information about the alarm type that was activated.
You need to implement a reply trail auditing solution.Which two actions should you perform? Each correct answer presents part of the solution. NOTE: Each correct selection is worth one point.Assign the value of the hazard message SessionID property to the ReplyToSessionId property.
G. Assign the value of the hazard message MessageId property to the DevileryCount property.
H. Assign the value of the hazard message SessionID property to the SequenceNumber property.
I. Assign the value of the hazard message MessageId property to the CorrelationId property.
J. Assign the value of the hazard message SequenceNumber property to the DeliveryCount property.
K. Assign the value of the hazard message MessageId property to the SequenceNumber property.
Answer: GJ

QUESTION 159

-
Note: This question is part of a series of questions that present the same scenario. Each question in the series contains a unique solution that might meet the stated goals. Some question sets might have more than one correct solution, while others might not have a correct solution.
After you answer a question in this section, you will NOT be able to return to it. As a result, these questions will not appear in the review screen.
You develop and deploy an Azure App Service API app to a Windows-hosted deployment slot named Development. You create additional deployment slots named Testing and Production. You enable auto swap on the Production deployment slot.
You need to ensure that scripts run and resources are available before a swap operation occurs.

Solution: Update the app with a method named statuscheck to run the scripts. Update the app settings for the app. Set the WEBSITE_SWAP_WARMUP_PING_PATH and WEBSITE_SWAP_WARMUP_PING_STATUSES with a path to the new method and appropriate response codes. Does the solution meet the goal?
C. Yes
D. No
Answer: B

QUESTION 160

-

A company is implementing a publish-subscribe (Pub/Sub) messaging component by using Azure Service Bus. You are developing the first subscription application.
In the Azure portal you see that messages are being sent to the subscription for each topic. You create and initialize a subscription client object by supplying the correct details, but the subscription application is still not consuming the messages.
You need to complete the source code of the subscription client What should you do?
E. await subscriptionClient.CloseAsync();
F. await subscriptionClient.AddRuleAsync(new RuleDescription(RuleDescription.DefaultRuleName, new TrueFilter()));
G. subscriptionClient.RegisterMessageHandler(ProcessMessagesAsync, messageHandlerOptions);
H. subscriptionClient = new SubscriptionClient(ServiceBusConnectionString, TopicName, SubscriptionName);
Answer: C

QUESTION 161

-

Note: This question is part of a series of questions that present the same scenario. Each question in the series contains a unique solution that might meet the stated goals. Some question sets might have more than one correct solution, while others might not have a correct solution.
After you answer a question in this section, you will NOT be able to return to it. As a result, these questions will not appear in the review screen.
You are developing a website that will run as an Azure Web App. Users will authenticate by using their Azure Active Directory (Azure AD) credentials.
You plan to assign users one of the following permission levels for the website: admin, normal, and reader. A user's Azure AD group membership must be used to determine the permission level.
You need to configure authorization. Solution:
Create a new Azure AD application. In the application's manifest, define application roles that match the required permission levels for the application. Assign the appropriate Azure AD group to each role. In the website, use the value of the roles claim from the JWT for the user to determine permissions. Does the solution meet the goal?
C. Yes
D. No
Answer: B

QUESTION 162

-

You have a single page application (SPA) web application that manages information based on data returned by Microsoft Graph from another company's Azure Active Directory (Azure AD) instance.
Users must be able to authenticate and access Microsoft Graph by using their own company's Azure AD instance. You need to configure the application manifest for the app registration.
How should you complete the manifest? To answer, select the appropriate options in the answer area. NOTE: Each correct selection is worth one point.
C. Mastered
D. Not Mastered
Answer: A

QUESTION 163

-

You are developing a new page for a website that uses Azure Cosmos DB for data storage. The feature uses documents that have the following format:
You must display data for the new page in a specific order. You create the following query for the page:
You need to configure a Cosmos DB policy to the support the query.
How should you configure the policy? To answer, drag the appropriate JSON segments to the correct locations. Each JSON segment may be used once, more than once, or not at all. You may need to drag the split bar between panes or scroll to view content.NOTE: Each correct selection is worth one point.
C. Mastered
D. Not Mastered
Answer: A

QUESTION 164

-

You are implementing an order processing system. A point of sale application publishes orders to topics in an Azure Service Bus queue. The label property for the topic includes the following data:
The system has the following requirements for subscriptions
You need to implement filtering and maximize throughput while evaluating filters.
Which filter types should you implement? To answer, drag the appropriate filter types to the correct subscriptions. Each filter type may be used once, more than once, or not at all. You may need to drag the split bar between panes or scroll to view content.
NOTE: Each correct selection is worth one point.
A. Mastered
B. Not Mastered
Answer: A

QUESTION 165

-

You are developing an ASP.NET Core website that can be used to manage photographs which are stored in Azure Blob Storage containers. Users of the website authenticate by using their Azure Active Directory (Azure AD) credentials.

You implement role-based access control (RBAC) role permission on the containers that store photographs. You assign users to RBAC role.

You need to configure the website's Azure AD Application so that user's permissions can be used with the Azure Blob containers.

How should you configure the application? To answer, drag the appropriate setting to the correct location. Each setting may be used once, more than once, or not at all. You may need to drag the split bar between panes or scroll to view content.

NOTE: Each correct selection is worth one point.

C. Mastered

D. Not Mastered

Answer: A

QUESTION 166

-

Note: This question is part of a series of questions that present the same scenario. Each question in the scries contains a unique solution that might meet the stated goals. Some question sets might have more than one correct solution, while others might not have a correct solution.After you answer a question in this section, you will NOT be able to return to it. As a result these questions will not appear in the review screen. Margie's Travel is an international travel and bookings management service. The company is expanding into restaurant bookings. You are tasked with implementing Azure Search for the restaurants listed in their solution.

You create the index in Azure Search.

You need to import the restaurant data into the Azure Search service by using the Azure Search .NET SDK. Solution:

* 1. Create a as object to connect to the search index.

* 2. Create a Data Container that contains the documents which must be added.

* 3. Create a Data Source instance and set its Container property to the DataContamer

* 4 Call the Documents. Suggest method of the as and pass the Data Source. Does the solution meet the goal?

C. Yes

D. No

Answer: B

QUESTION 167

-

Note: This question is part of a series of questions that present the same scenario. Each question in the series contains a unique solution that might meet the stated goals. Some question sets might have more than one correct solution, while others might not have a correct solution.

After you answer a question in this section, you will NOT be able to return to it. As a result, these questions will not appear in the review screen.

You develop a software as a service (SaaS) offering to manage photographs. Users upload photos to a web service which then stores the photos in Azure Storage Blob storage. The storage account type is

General-purpose V2.

When photos are uploaded, they must be processed to produce and save a mobile-friendly version of the image. The process to produce a mobile-friendly version of the image must start in less than one minute.

You need to design the process that starts the photo processing.
Solution: Move photo processing to an Azure Function triggered from the blob upload. Does the solution meet the goal?
C. Yes
D. No
Answer: A

QUESTION 168

-

You are developing a web service that will run on Azure virtual machines that use Azure Storage. You configure all virtual machines to use managed identities. You have the following requirements:
Must use only Azure Instance Metadata Service endpoints.
You need to write code to retrieve an access token to access Azure Storage. To answer, drag the appropriate code segments to the correct locations. Each code segment may be used once or not at all. You may need to drag the split bar between panes or scroll to view content.
NOTE: Each correct selection is worth one point.
C. Mastered
D. Not Mastered
Answer: A

QUESTION 169

-

Note: This question is part of a series of questions that present the same scenario. Each question in the series contains a unique solution. Determine whether the solution meets the stated goals.
You are developing and deploying several ASP.Net web applications to Azure App Service. You plan to save session state information and HTML output. You must use a storage mechanism with the following requirements:
•Share session state across all ASP.NET web applications
•Support controlled, concurrent access to the same session state data for multiple readers and a single writer
•Save full HTTP responses for concurrent requests You need to store the information.
Proposed Solution: Deploy and configure an Azure Database for PostgreSQL. Update the web applications. Does the solution meet the goal?
C. Yes
D. No
Answer: D

QUESTION 170

-

You have an existing Azure storage account that stores large volumes of data across multiple containers. You need to copy all data from the existing storage account to a new storage account. The copy process must meet the following requirements:
Automate data movement.
Minimize user input required to perform the operation. Ensure that the data movement process is recoverable. What should you use?

A. AZ Copy
B. Azure Storage Explorer
C. Azure portal
D. .NET Storage Client Library
Answer: A

QUESTION 171

-

You are developing an Azure App Service REST API.
The API must be called by an Azure App Service web app. The API must retrieve and update user profile information stored in Azure Active Directory (Azure AD). You need to configure the API to make the updates.
Which two tools should you use? Each correct answer presents part of the solution. NOTE: Each correct selection is worth one point.
A. Microsoft Graph API
B. Microsoft Authentication Library (MSAL)
C. Azure API Management
D. Microsoft Azure Security Center
E. Microsoft Azure Key Vault SDK
Answer: AC

QUESTION 172

-

You plan to deploy a new application to a Linux virtual machine (VM) that is hosted in Azure.
The entire VM must be secured at rest by using industry-standard encryption technology to address organizational security and compliance requirements. You need to configure Azure Disk Encryption for the VM.
How should you complete the Azure Cli commands? To answer, select the appropriate options in the answer area. NOTE: Each correct selection is worth one point.
A. Mastered
B. Not Mastered
Answer: A

QUESTION 173

-

You are developing a data storage solution for a social networking app.
The solution requires a mobile app that stores user information using Azure Table Storage. You need to develop code that can insert multiple sets of user information.
How should you complete the code? To answer, select the appropriate options in the answer area. NOTE: Each correct selection is worth one point.
A. Mastered
B. Not Mastered
Answer: A

QUESTION 174

-

Note: This question is part of a series of questions that present the same scenario. Each question in the series contains a unique solution that might meet the stated goals. Some question sets might have more than one correct solution, while others might not have a correct solution.
After you answer a question in this section, you will NOT be able to return to it. As a result, these questions will not appear in the review screen.
You develop and deploy an Azure App Service API app to a Windows-hosted deployment slot named Development. You create additional deployment slots named Testing and Production. You enable auto swap on the Production deployment slot.
You need to ensure that scripts run and resources are available before a swap operation occurs.
Solution: Enable auto swap for the Testing slot. Deploy the app to the Testing slot.
Does the solution meet the goal?
A. Yes
B . No
Answer: B

QUESTION 175

-

You need to configure Azure CDN for the Shipping web site.
Which configuration options should you use? To answer, select the appropriate options in the answer area. NOTE: Each correct selection is worth one point.

Option	Value
Tier	I. Standard II Premium
Profile	I Akamai II Microsoft
Optimization	I. General web delivery II. Large file download III. Dynamic site acceleration IV Video-on-demand media streaming

A. Mastered
B. Not Mastered
Answer: A

QUESTION 176

-

You need to configure Azure App Service to support the REST API requirements.
Which values should you use? To answer, select the appropriate options in the answer area. NOTE: Each correct selection is worth one point.

Setting	Value
Plan	1. Basic 2. Standard 3. Premium 4. Isolated
Instance Count	1. 1 2. 10 3. 20 4. 100

A. Mastered
B. Not Mastered
Answer: A

QUESTION 177

-

You need to correct the VM issues.
Which tools should you use? To answer, select the appropriate options in the answer area. NOTE: Each correct selection is worth one point.

Issue	Tool
Backup and restore	1. Azure Site Recovery 2. Azure Backup 3. Azure Data Box 4. Azure Migrate
Performance	1. Azure Network Watcher 2. Azure Traffic Manager 3. ExpressRoute 4. Accelerated Networking

A. Mastered
B. Not Mastered
Answer: A

QUESTION 178

-

Note: This question is part of a series of questions that present the same scenario. Each question in the series contains a unique solution that might meet the stated goals. Some question sets might have more than one correct solution, while others might not have a correct solution.
After you answer a question in this question, you will NOT be able to return to it. As a result, these questions will not appear in the review screen. You are developing a website that will run as an Azure Web App. Users will authenticate by using their Azure Active Directory (Azure AD) credentials.
You plan to assign users one of the following permission levels for the website: admin, normal, and reader. A user's Azure AD group membership must be used to determine the permission level.
You need to configure authorization.
Solution: Configure the Azure Web App for the website to allow only authenticated requests and require Azure AD log on. Does the solution meet the goal?
A. Yes
B. No
Answer: B

QUESTION 179

-

Note: This question is part of a series of questions that present the same scenario. Each question in the series contains a unique solution. Determine whether the solution meets the stated goals.
You are developing and deploying several ASP.Net web applications to Azure App Service. You plan to save session state information and HTML output. You must use a storage mechanism with the following requirements:
•Share session state across all ASP.NET web applications
•Support controlled, concurrent access to the same session state data for multiple readers and a single writer
•Save full HTTP responses for concurrent requests You need to store the information.
Proposed Solution: Add the web applications to Docker containers. Deploy the containers. Deploy the containers to Azure Kubernetes Service (AKS). Does the solution meet the goal?

A. Yes
B. No
Answer: B

QUESTION 180

-

You are developing a project management service by using ASP.NET. The service hosts conversations, files, to-do lists, and a calendar that users can interact with at any time.
The application uses Azure Search for allowing users to search for keywords in the project data.
You need to implement code that creates the object which is used to create indexes in the Azure Search service.
Which two objects should you use? Each correct answer presents part of the solution. NOTE: Each correct selection is worth one point.
A. Search Service
B. Search Service
C. Search Service
D. Search Credentials
Answer: BC

QUESTION 181

-

You develop a web app that uses tier D1 app service plan by using the Web Apps feature of Microsoft Azure App Service. Spikes in traffic have caused increases in page load times.
You need to ensure that the web app automatically scales when CPU load is about 85 percent and minimize costs.
Which four actions should you perform in sequence? To answer, move the appropriate actions from the list of actions to the answer area and arrange them in the correct order.
NOTE: More than one order of answer choices is correct. You will receive credit for any of the correct orders you select.

Actions
1Configure the web app to the Premium App Service tier.
2. Configure the web app to the Standard App Service tier.
3. Enable autoscaling on the web app.
4. Add a scale rule.
5. Switch to an azure plan Service consumption plan.

A. Mastered
B. Not Mastered
Answer: A

QUESTION 182

-

Note: This question is part of a series of questions that present the same scenario. Each question in the series contains a unique solution that might meet the stated goals. Some question sets might have more than one correct solution, while others might not have a correct solution.

After you answer a question in this section, you will NOT be able to return to it. As a result, these questions will not appear in the review screen. Margie's Travel is an international travel and bookings management service. The company is expanding into restaurant bookings. You are tasked with implementing Azure Search tor the restaurants listed in their solution.
You create the index in Azure Search.
You need to import the restaurant data into the Azure Search service by using the Azure Search NET SDK. Solution:
* 1. Create a Search Service object to connect to the search index.
* 2. Create a Data Container that contains the documents which must be added.
* 3. Create a Data Source instance and set its Container property to the Data Container.
* 4. Set the Data Source property of the SearchServiceClient Does the solution meet the goal?
A. Yes
B. No
Answer: B

QUESTION 183

-

Note: This question is part of a series of questions that present the same scenario. Each question in the series contains a unique solution that might meet the stated goals. Some question sets might have more than one correct solution, while others might not have a correct solution.
After you answer a question in this section, you will NOT be able to return to it. As a result, these questions will not appear in the review screen.
You are developing an Azure solution to collect point-of-sale (POS) device data from 2,000 stores located throughout the world. A single device can produce 2 megabytes (MB) of data every 24 hours. Each store location has one to five devices that send data.
You must store the device data in Azure Blob storage. Device data must be correlated based on a device identifier. Additional stores are expected to open in the future.
You need to implement a solution to receive the device data.
Solution: Provision an Azure Service Bus. Configure a topic to receive the device data by using a correlation filter. Does the solution meet the goal?
A. Yes
B. No
Answer: A

QUESTION 184

-

You develop and deploy a Java RESTful API to Azure App Service.
You open a browser and navigate to the URL for the API. You receive the following error message: Failed to load 'http://api.azurewebsites.net:6000/#/api/Products:NoControl-Allow-Origin'header is present on the requested resource. Origin 'http://localhost:6000' is therefore not allowed access.
You need to resolve the error.
What should you do?
A. Bind an SSL certificate
B. Enable authentication
C. Enable CORS
D. Map a custom domain

E. Add a CDN

Answer: C

QUESTION 185

-

You are preparing to deploy a medical records application to an Azure virtual machine (VM). The application will be deployed by using a VHD produced by an on- premises build server.

You need to ensure that both the application and related data are encrypted during and after deployment to Azure.

Which three actions should you perform in sequence? To answer, move the appropriate actions from the list of actions to the answer area and arrange them in the correct order.

Actions
Encrypt the on-premises VHD by using BitLocker without a TPM, Upload the VM to Azure Storage.
Run the Azure PowerShell command set-AzureRmVMDiskEncryptionExtension.
Run the Azure PowerShell command Set-AzureRmVMOSDisk.
Encrypt the on-premises VHD by using BitLocker with a TPM. Upload the VM to Azure Storage.
Run the Azure PowerShell Command New-AzureRmVM.

A. Mastered

B. Not Mastered

Answer: A

QUESTION 186

-

You are developing an ASP.NET Core Web API web service. The web service uses Azure Application Insights for all telemetry and dependency tracking. The web service reads and writes data to a database other than Microsoft SQL Server.

You need to ensure that dependency tracking works for calls to the third-party database.

Which two Dependency Telemetry properties should you store in the database? Each correct answer presents part of the solution. NOTE: Each correct selection is worth one point.

Answer area
Encrypt the on-premises VHD by using BitLocker without a TPM. Upload the VM to Azure Storage.
Run the Azure PowerShell command set-AzureRmVMDSDisk.
Run the Azure PowerShell command set-AzureRmVMDiskEncryptionExtension.

A. Telemetry.Context.Operation.Id
B. Tetemetry.Context.Cloud.Rolelnstance
C. Telemetry.Id
D. Telemetry.ContextSession.Id
E. Telemetry.Name
Answer: AC

QUESTION 187

-

Your company is developing an Azure API.
You need to implement authentication for the Azure API. You have the following requirements:
All API calls must be secure.
Callers to the API must not send credentials to the API. Which authentication mechanism should you use?
A. Basic
B. Anonymous
C. Managed identity
D. Client certificate
Answer: C

QUESTION 188

-

Note: This question is part of a series of questions that present the same scenario. Each question in the series contains a unique solution that might meet the stated goals. Some question sets might have more than one correct solution, while others might not have a correct solution.
After you answer a question in this section, you will NOT be able to return to it. As a result, these questions will not appear in the review screen.
You develop a software as a service (SaaS) offering to manage photographs. Users upload photos to a web service which then stores the photos in Azure Storage Blob storage. The storage account type is
General-purpose V2.
When photos are uploaded, they must be processed to produce and save a mobile-friendly version of the image. The process to produce a mobile-friendly version of the image must start in less than one minute.
You need to design the process that starts the photo processing.
Solution: Move photo processing to an Azure Function triggered from the blob upload. Does the solution meet the goal?
A. Yes
B. No
Answer: A

QUESTION 189

-

You are preparing to deploy an ASP.NET Core website to an Azure Web App from a GitHub repository. The website includes static content generated by a script. You plan to use the Azure Web App continuous deployment feature.
You need to run the static generation script before the website starts serving traffic.
What are two possible ways to achieve this goal? Each correct answer presents a complete solution.
NOTE: Each correct selection is worth one point.
A. Create a file named .deployment in the root of the repository that calls a script which generates the static content and deploys the website.
B. Add a PreBuild target in the websites csproj project file that runs the static content generation script.
C. Create a file named run.cmd in the folder /run that calls a script which generates the static content and deploys the website.
D. Add the path to the static content generation tool to WEBSITE_RUN_FROM_PACKAGE setting in the host.json file.
Answer: AD

QUESTION 190

-

Note: This question is part of a series of questions that present the same scenario. Each question in the series contains a unique solution that might meet the stated goals. Some question sets might have more than one correct solution, while others might not have a correct solution.
After you answer a question in this section, you will NOT be able to return to it. As a result, these questions will not appear in the review screen.
You develop a software as a service (SaaS) offering to manage photographs. Users upload photos to a web service which then stores the photos in Azure Storage Blob storage. The storage account type is
General-purpose V2.
When photos are uploaded, they must be processed to produce and save a mobile-friendly version of the image. The process to produce a mobile-friendly version of the image must start in less than one minute.
You need to design the process that starts the photo processing.
Solution: Convert the Azure Storage account to a BlockBlobStorage storage account. Does the solution meet the goal?
C. Yes
D. No
Answer: B

QUESTION 191

-

Note: This question is part of a series of questions that present the same scenario. Each question in the series contains a unique solution that might meet the stated goals. Some question sets might have more than one correct solution, while others might not have a correct solution.
After you answer a question in this question, you will NOT be able to return to it. As a result, these questions will not appear in the review screen. You are developing a website that will run as an Azure Web App. Users will authenticate by using their Azure Active Directory (Azure AD) credentials.

You plan to assign users one of the following permission levels for the website: admin, normal, and reader. A user's Azure AD group membership must be used to determine the permission level. You need to configure authorization.
Solution:
•Create a new Azure AD application's manifest, set value of the groupMembershipClaims option to All.
•In the website, use the value of the groups claim from the JWI for the user to determine permissions. Does the solution meet the goal?
C. Yes
D. No
Answer: A

QUESTION 192
-You are writing code to create and run an Azure Batch job. You have created a pool of compute nodes.
You need to choose the right class and its method to submit a batch job to the Batch service. Which method should you use?
A. JobOperations.CreateJobO
B. CloudJob.Enable(I Enumerable<I Enumerable>)
C. CloudJob.CommitAsync(I Enumerable<I Enumerable>, Cancellation Token)
D. JobOperations.EnableJob(String, I Enumerable<I Enumerable>)
E. JobOperations.EnableJobAsync(Strin
F. I Enumerable<I Enumerable>. Cancellation Token)
Answer: C

QUESTION 193
-
You are developing a software solution for an autonomous transportation system. The solution uses large data sets and Azure Batch processing to simulate navigation sets for entire fleets of vehicles.
You need to create compute nodes for the solution on Azure Batch. What should you do?
A. In Python, implement the class: as
B. In Python, implement the class: as
C. In the Azure portal, create a Batch account
D. In a .NET method, call the method: BatchClient.PoolOperations.CreateJob
Answer: D

QUESTION 194
-
You have an Azure App Services Web App. Azure SQL Database instance. Azure Storage Account and an Azure Redis Cache instance in a resource group. A developer must be able to publish code to the web app. You must grant the developer the Contribute role to the web app
You need to grant the role.
What two commands can you use? Each correct answer presents a complete solution. NOTE: Each correct selection is worth one point.
A. New-Cancellation Token

B. as role assignment create
C. as role definition create
D. New-as
Answer: AB

QUESTION 195

-

Note: This question is part of a series of questions that present the same scenario. Each question in the series contains a unique solution that might meet the stated goals. Some question sets might have more than one correct solution, while others might not have a correct solution.
After you answer a question in this section, you will NOT be able to return to it. As a result, these questions will not appear in the review screen.
You are developing an Azure Service application that processes queue data when it receives a message from a mobile application. Messages may not be sent to the service consistently.
You have the following requirements:
Queue size must not grow larger than 80 gigabytes (GB).
Use first-in-first-out (FIFO) ordering of messages. Minimize Azure costs.
You need to implement the messaging solution.
Solution: Use the .Net API to add a message to an Azure Service Bus Queue from the mobile application. Create an Azure Function App that uses an Azure Service Bus Queue trigger.
Does the solution meet the goal?
A. Yes
B. No
Answer: A

QUESTION 196

-

You develop an Azure web app. You monitor performance of the web app by using Application Insights. You need to ensure the cost for Application Insights does not exceed a preset budget. What should you do?
A. Implement ingestion sampling using the Azure portal.
B. Set a daily cap for the Application Insights instance.
C. Implement adaptive sampling using the Azure portal.
D. Implement adaptive sampling using the Application Insights SDK.
E. Implement ingestion sampling using the Application Insights SDK.
Answer: D

QUESTION 197

-

Note: This question is part of a series of questions that present the same scenario. Each question in the series contains a unique solution that might meet the stated goals. Some question sets might have more than one correct solution, while others might not have a correct solution.
After you answer a question in this section, you will NOT be able to return to it. As a result, these questions will not appear in the review screen. Margie's Travel is an international travel and bookings management service. The company is expanding into restaurant bookings. You are

tasked with implementing Azure Search for the restaurants listed in their solution You create the index in Azure Search.

You need to import the restaurant data into the Azure Search service by using the Azure Search NET SDK. Solution:

* 1 Create a as object to connect to the search index
* 2. Create an Index Batch that contains the documents which must be added.
* 3. Call the Documents. Index method of the Documents. Index and pass the Index Batch.. Does the solution meet the goal?

A. Yes

B. No

Answer: A

QUESTION 198

-

You develop Azure solutions.

You must connect to a No-SQL globally-distributed database by using the .NET API. You need to create an object to configure and execute requests in the database. Which code segment should you use?

A. new Container(EndpointUri, PrimaryKey);

B. new Database(Endpoint, PrimaryKey);

C. new CosmosClient(EndpointUri, PrimaryKey);

Answer: C

QUESTION 199

-

You are creating a hazard notification system that has a single signaling server which triggers audio and visual alarms to start and stop.

You implement Azure Service Bus to publish alarms. Each alarm controller uses Azure Service Bus to receive alarm signals as part of a transaction. Alarm events must be recorded for audit purposes. Each transaction record must include information about the alarm type that was activated.

You need to implement a reply trail auditing solution.

Which two actions should you perform? Each correct answer presents part of the solution. NOTE: Each correct selection is worth one point.

A. Assign the value of the hazard message SessionID property to the SequenceNumber property.

B. Assign the value of the hazard message SequenceNumber property to the DeliveryCount propert

C. Assign the value of the hazard message Messageld property to the DeliveryCount property.

D. Assign the value of the hazard message SessionID property to the ReplyToSessionld property.

E. Assign the value of the hazard message Messageld property to the SequenceNumber property.

F. Assign the value of the hazard message Messageld property to the Correlationld property.

Answer: AB

QUESTION 200

-

Note: This question is part of a series of questions that present the same scenario. Each question in the series contains a unique solution that might meet the stated goals. Some question sets might have more than one correct solution, while others might not have a correct solution.

After you answer a question in this question, you will NOT be able to return to it. As a result, these questions will not appear in the review screen. You are developing a website that will run as an Azure Web App. Users will authenticate by using their Azure Active Directory (Azure AD) credentials.
You plan to assign users one of the following permission levels for the website: admin, normal, and reader. A user's Azure AD group membership must be used to determine the permission level.
You need to configure authorization.
Solution: Configure the Azure Web App for the website to allow only authenticated requests and require Azure AD log on. Does the solution meet the goal?
A. Yes
B. No
Answer: B

QUESTION 201

-
Note: This question is part of a series of questions that present the same scenario. Each question in the series contains a unique solution. Determine whether the solution meets the stated goals.
You are developing and deploying several ASP.Net web applications to Azure App Service. You plan to save session state information and HTML output. You must use a storage mechanism with the following requirements:
•Share session state across all ASP.NET web applications
•Support controlled, concurrent access to the same session state data for multiple readers and a single writer
•Save full HTTP responses for concurrent requests You need to store the information.
Proposed Solution: Add the web applications to Docker containers. Deploy the containers. Deploy the containers to Azure Kubernetes Service (AKS). Does the solution meet the goal?
A. Yes
B. No
Answer: B

QUESTION 202

-
You are developing a project management service by using ASP.NET. The service hosts conversations, files, to-do lists, and a calendar that users can interact with at any time.
The application uses Azure Search for allowing users to search for keywords in the project data.
You need to implement code that creates the object which is used to create indexes in the Azure Search service.
Which two objects should you use? Each correct answer presents part of the solution. NOTE: Each correct selection is worth one point.
A. Search Service
B. Search Service
C. Search Service
D. Search Credentials
Answer: BC

QUESTION 203

-

Note: This question is part of a series of questions that present the same scenario. Each question in the series contains a unique solution that might meet the stated goals. Some question sets might have more than one correct solution, while others might not have a correct solution.

After you answer a question in this section, you will NOT be able to return to it. As a result, these questions will not appear in the review screen. Margie's Travel is an international travel and bookings management service. The company is expanding into restaurant bookings. You are tasked with implementing Azure Search tor the restaurants listed in their solution.

You create the index in Azure Search.

You need to import the restaurant data into the Azure Search service by using the Azure Search NET SDK. Solution:

* 1. Create a Search Service object to connect to the search index.
* 2. Create a Data Container that contains the documents which must be added.
* 3. Create a Data Source instance and set its Container property to the Data Container.
* 4. Set the Data Source property of the SearchServiceClient Does the solution meet the goal?

A. Yes

B. No

Answer: B

QUESTION 204

-

Note: This question is part of a series of questions that present the same scenario. Each question in the series contains a unique solution that might meet the stated goals. Some question sets might have more than one correct solution, while others might not have a correct solution.

After you answer a question in this section, you will NOT be able to return to it. As a result, these questions will not appear in the review screen.

You are developing an Azure solution to collect point-of-sale (POS) device data from 2,000 stores located throughout the world. A single device can produce 2 megabytes (MB) of data every 24 hours. Each store location has one to five devices that send data.

You must store the device data in Azure Blob storage. Device data must be correlated based on a device identifier. Additional stores are expected to open in the future.

You need to implement a solution to receive the device data.

Solution: Provision an Azure Service Bus. Configure a topic to receive the device data by using a correlation filter. Does the solution meet the goal?

A. Yes

B. No

Answer: A

QUESTION 205

-

You develop and deploy a Java RESTful API to Azure App Service.

You open a browser and navigate to the URL for the API. You receive the following error message:

```
Failed to load http://api.azurewebsites.net:6000/#/api/Products: No 'Access-
Control-Allow-Origin'header is present on the requested resource.
Origin 'http://localhost:6000' is therefore not allowed access
```

You need to resolve the error.
What should you do?
A. Bind an SSL certificate
B. Enable authentication
C. Enable CORS
D. Map a custom domain
E. Add a CDN
Answer: C

QUESTION 206

-

You are developing an ASP.NET Core Web API web service. The web service uses Azure Application Insights for all telemetry and dependency tracking. The web service reads and writes data to a database other than Microsoft SQL Server.
You need to ensure that dependency tracking works for calls to the third-party database.
Which two Dependency Telemetry properties should you store in the database? Each correct answer presents part of the solution. NOTE: Each correct selection is worth one point.
A. Telemetry.Context.Operation.Id
B. Tetemetry.Context.Cloud.Rolelnstance
C. Telemetry.Id
D. Telemetry.ContextSession.Id
E. Telemetry.Name
Answer: AC

QUESTION 207

-

Your company is developing an Azure API.
You need to implement authentication for the Azure API. You have the following requirements:
All API calls must be secure.
Callers to the API must not send credentials to the API. Which authentication mechanism should you use?
A. Basic
B. Anonymous
C. Managed identity
D. Client certificate
Answer: C

QUESTION 208

-

Note: This question is part of a series of questions that present the same scenario. Each question in the series contains a unique solution that might meet the stated goals. Some question sets might have more than one correct solution, while others might not have a correct solution.
After you answer a question in this section, you will NOT be able to return to it. As a result, these questions will not appear in the review screen.

You develop a software as a service (SaaS) offering to manage photographs. Users upload photos to a web service which then stores the photos in Azure Storage Blob storage. The storage account type is
General-purpose V2.
When photos are uploaded, they must be processed to produce and save a mobile-friendly version of the image. The process to produce a mobile-friendly version of the image must start in less than one minute.
You need to design the process that starts the photo processing.
Solution: Move photo processing to an Azure Function triggered from the blob upload. Does the solution meet the goal?
A. Yes
B. No
Answer: A

QUESTION 209

-

You are developing an application that uses Azure Storage Queues. You have the following code:
CloudStorageAccount storage Account = CloudstorageAccount. Parse
(CloudConfigurationManager.GetSetting("StorageConnectionString"));
CloudQueueClient queue Client = storageAccount.CreateCloudQueueClient()

CloudQueue queue = queueClient.GetQueueReference ("appqueue");
await queue. CreateIfNotExistsAsync ();

CloudQueueMessage peeked Message = await queue. PeekMessageAsync ();
if (peekedMessage! = null)
{
Console. WriteLine ("The peeked message is: {0}", peekedMessage.AsString);
}
CloudQueueMessage message = await queue. GetMessageAsync ();
For each of the following statements, select Yes if the statement is true. Otherwise, select No.
NOTE: Each correct selection is worth one point.

Statement	Yes/No
The code configures the lock duration for the queue.	No
The last message read remains in the queue after the code runs.	Yes
The storage queue remains in the storage account after the code runs.	Yes

A. Mastered
B. Not Mastered
Answer: A

QUESTION 210

-

You are preparing to deploy an ASP.NET Core website to an Azure Web App from a GitHub repository. The website includes static content generated by a script. You plan to use the Azure Web App continuous deployment feature.
You need to run the static generation script before the website starts serving traffic.
What are two possible ways to achieve this goal? Each correct answer presents a complete solution.
NOTE: Each correct selection is worth one point.
A. Create a file named .deployment in the root of the repository that calls a script which generates the static content and deploys the website.
B. Add a PreBuild target in the websites csproj project file that runs the static content generation script.
C. Create a file named run.cmd in the folder /run that calls a script which generates the static content and deploys the website.
D. Add the path to the static content generation tool to WEBSITE_RUN_FROM_PACKAGE setting in the host.json file.
Answer: AD

QUESTION 211

-
Note: This question is part of a series of questions that present the same scenario. Each question in the series contains a unique solution that might meet the stated goals. Some question sets might have more than one correct solution, while others might not have a correct solution.
After you answer a question in this section, you will NOT be able to return to it. As a result, these questions will not appear in the review screen.
You develop a software as a service (SaaS) offering to manage photographs. Users upload photos to a web service which then stores the photos in Azure Storage Blob storage. The storage account type is
General-purpose V2.
When photos are uploaded, they must be processed to produce and save a mobile-friendly version of the image. The process to produce a mobile-friendly version of the image must start in less than one minute.
You need to design the process that starts the photo processing.
Solution: Convert the Azure Storage account to a BlockBlobStorage storage account. Does the solution meet the goal?
A. Yes
B. No
Answer: B

QUESTION 212

Note: This question is part of a series of questions that present the same scenario. Each question in the series contains a unique solution that might meet the stated goals. Some question sets might have more than one correct solution, while others might not have a correct solution.
After you answer a question in this question, you will NOT be able to return to it. As a result, these questions will not appear in the review screen. You are developing a website that will run as an Azure Web App. Users will authenticate by using their Azure Active Directory (Azure AD) credentials.

You plan to assign users one of the following permission levels for the website: admin, normal, and reader. A user's Azure AD group membership must be used to determine the permission level. You need to configure authorization.
Solution:
•Create a new Azure AD application's manifest, set value of the groupMembershipClaims option to All.
•In the website, use the value of the groups claim from the JWI for the user to determine permissions. Does the solution meet the goal?
A. Yes
B. No
Answer: A

QUESTION 213

-

You develop an ASP.NET Core MVC application. You configure the application to track webpages and custom events. You need to identify trends in application usage.
Which Azure Application Insights Usage Analysis features should you use? To answer, drag the appropriate features to the correct requirements. Each feature may be used once, more than once, or not at all. You may need to drag the split bar between panes or scroll to view content.
NOTE: Each correct selection is worth one point.

Requirement	Feature
Which pages visited by users most often correlate to a product purchase?	Users
How does load time of the product display page affect a user's decision to purchase a product?	Impact
Which events most influence a user's decision to continue to use the application?	Retentions
Are there places in the application that users often perform repetitive actions?	User flows

A. Mastered
B. Not Mastered
Answer: A

QUESTION 214

-

You are writing code to create and run an Azure Batch job. You have created a pool of compute nodes.
You need to choose the right class and its method to submit a batch job to the Batch service. Which method should you use?
A. JobOperations.CreateJobO
B. CloudJob.Enable(I Enumerable<I Enumerable>)
C. CloudJob.CommitAsync(I Enumerable<I Enumerable>, Cancellation Token)
D. JobOperations.EnableJob(String, I Enumerable<I Enumerable>)
E. JobOperations.EnableJobAsync(Strin
F. I Enumerable<I Enumerable>. Cancellation Token)
Answer: C

QUESTION 215

-

You are developing a software solution for an autonomous transportation system. The solution uses large data sets and Azure Batch processing to simulate navigation sets for entire fleets of vehicles.

You need to create compute nodes for the solution on Azure Batch. What should you do?

A. In Python, implement the class: as

B. In Python, implement the class: as

C. In the Azure portal, create a Batch account

D. In a .NET method, call the method: BatchClient.PoolOperations.CreateJob

Answer: D

QUESTION 216

-

You have an Azure App Services Web App. Azure SQL Database instance. Azure Storage Account and an Azure Redis Cache instance in a resource group. A developer must be able to publish code to the web app. You must grant the developer the Contribute role to the web app

You need to grant the role.

What two commands can you use? Each correct answer presents a complete solution. NOTE: Each correct selection is worth one point.

A. New-Cancellation Token

B. as role assignment create

C. as role definition create

D. New-as

Answer: AB

ONLINE RESOURCES

Practice Paper

Link : https://forms.gle/urKhdNP8PSGcBfYf9

QR Code :

Video Content

Link :

https://www.youtube.com/playlist?list=PLzlh_31VWEFqT72UPVCUi6rqRqLBuwMSr

QR Code :

Chapter 3: Viva Voce Questions

Q 1: What is the primary focus of the Azure Developer AZ-204 certification?
Answer: The AZ-204 certification focuses on the development of solutions that use Azure services, including compute, network, storage, and security.
Q 2: How do Azure Functions enhance serverless computing?
Answer: Azure Functions allow developers to run code in response to triggers such as timers or HTTP requests without managing infrastructure, simplifying serverless application development.
Q 3: What role does Azure Logic Apps play in application integration?
Answer: Azure Logic Apps provides a visual designer to orchestrate data flows and integrate services, apps, and systems, enabling automated workflows across different services.
Q 4: Can you explain the use of containers in Azure?
Answer: Containers in Azure, managed via Azure Kubernetes Service (AKS) and Azure Container Instances (ACI), provide lightweight, virtualized environments for applications, ensuring consistency across development, testing, and production environments.
Q 5: What is Azure DevOps?
Answer: Azure DevOps offers developer services to support teams to plan work, collaborate on code development, and build and deploy applications.
Q 6: How does Azure manage identity and access management?
Answer: Azure uses Azure Active Directory (AD) for identity services, providing single sign-on, multi-factor authentication, and management of users and groups.
Q 7: Describe how Azure Storage solutions are used in development.
Answer: Azure Storage provides scalable cloud storage for data objects, file systems, messaging stores, and NoSQL stores, crucial for applications requiring scalable, durable, and secure storage.
Q 8: What is an Azure Resource Manager template?
Answer: Azure Resource Manager templates are JSON files that define the resources needed for your application, enabling consistent deployments across different environments.
Q 9: How does Azure support IoT application development?
Answer: Azure IoT Hub allows developers to connect, monitor, and manage billions of IoT assets, while Azure IoT Central offers a fully managed global IoT SaaS solution for rapid development.
Q 10: Explain the concept of Azure Event Grid.
Answer: Azure Event Grid is a fully-managed event routing service which simplifies event-based app building with scalable event handling capabilities.
Q 11: What are Azure Cognitive Services?
Answer: Azure Cognitive Services are APIs that enable natural and contextual interaction within applications, using machine learning algorithms to process images, text, speech, and more.
Q 12: Describe the deployment strategies in Azure.
Answer: Azure supports various deployment strategies including blue-green, canary, and rolling deployments, allowing developers to manage updates with minimal downtime.
Q 13: What is Azure SignalR Service?
Answer: Azure SignalR Service simplifies the process of adding real-time web functionalities to applications over HTTP, enabling server-to-client streaming of content.
Q 14: How do you secure applications in Azure?
Answer: Security in Azure involves using Azure Security Center, integrating Azure AD, employing network security groups, and encrypting data in transit and at rest.
Q 15: What is Azure Cache for Redis?

Answer: Azure Cache for Redis provides a secure, dedicated cache service for high-throughput and low-latency data access needs, improving the performance of applications.

Q 16: How does Azure Service Bus facilitate communication?

Answer: Azure Service Bus is a fully managed enterprise integration message broker, facilitating secure and reliable communication across distributed applications.

Q 17: What is the use of Azure API Management?

Answer: Azure API Management allows organizations to publish APIs to external, partner, and internal developers to unlock the potential of their data and services.

Q 18: Explain data integration in Azure.

Answer: Data integration in Azure is facilitated by Azure Data Factory and Azure Synapse Analytics, which help in orchestrating and automating data movement and data transformation.

Q 19: What development tools are supported by Azure?

Answer: Azure supports a range of development tools including Visual Studio, VS Code, Eclipse, and more, providing integrations that enhance productivity.

Q 20: How does Azure support mobile app development?

Answer: Azure offers mobile app development services like Azure App Service, Notification Hubs, and Mobile Apps feature of App Service for backend, push notifications, and data synchronization.

YouTube Link for Viva Voce Questions:
https://www.youtube.com/playlist?list=PLzlh_31VWEFqT72UPVCUi6rqRqLBuwMSr

QR Code:

YouTube Videos Playlists for all Microsoft Certifications Videos

Microsoft Azure AI Fundamentals AZ-900
Link: https://www.youtube.com/playlist?list=PLzlh_31VWEFq9KU8Gr0ISbfj-TW6k17f8

QR Code:

Microsoft Azure Administrator AZ-104 Microsoft Azure Virtual Desktop AZ-140
Link: https://www.youtube.com/playlist?list=PLzlh_31VWEFq7JHJMuPJZcw-XShaPrUYP

QR Code:

Microsoft Azure Virtual Desktop AZ-140
Link: https://www.youtube.com/playlist?list=PLzlh_31VWEFowmPK_ro41wiljGoGKexGI

QR Code:

Microsoft Azure Developer AZ-204
Link:
https://www.youtube.com/playlist?list=PLzlh_31VWEFqT72UPVCUi6rqRqLBuwMSr

QR Code:

Designing Microsoft Azure Infrastructure Solution AZ-305
Link:
https://www.youtube.com/playlist?list=PLzlh_31VWEFpTerOknh9kgL4eTbhQwDND

QR Code:

Microsoft Azure Devops Engineer AZ-400
Link: https://www.youtube.com/playlist?list=PLzlh_31VWEFpyUIe_DuaeIkcThEfMT_BT

QR Code:

Microsoft Azure Security Engineer AZ-500
Link:
https://www.youtube.com/playlist?list=PLzlh_31VWEFqFBJgQTPNucIO0wVJdjNmS

QR Code:

Microsoft Azure Network Engineer AZ-700
Link:
https://www.youtube.com/playlist?list=PLzlh_31VWEFowujgDl16YDCvsQtmKgEqL

QR Code:

Microsoft Azure Fundamentals AZ-900
Link: https://www.youtube.com/playlist?list=PLzlh_31VWEFpeXZ2p32R1zDsgcbV8kI1K

QR Code: